T0311691

Cambridge Elements ☰

Elements in Beckett Studies
edited by
Dirk Van Hulle
University of Oxford
Mark Nixon
University of Reading

BECKETT AND STEIN

Georgina Nugent
University of Vienna

Shaftesbury Road, Cambridge CB2 8EA, United Kingdom

One Liberty Plaza, 20th Floor, New York, NY 10006, USA

477 Williamstown Road, Port Melbourne, VIC 3207, Australia

314–321, 3rd Floor, Plot 3, Splendor Forum, Jasola District Centre,
New Delhi – 110025, India

103 Penang Road, #05–06/07, Visioncrest Commercial, Singapore 238467

Cambridge University Press is part of Cambridge University Press & Assessment,
a department of the University of Cambridge.

We share the University's mission to contribute to society through the pursuit of
education, learning and research at the highest international levels of excellence.

www.cambridge.org
Information on this title: www.cambridge.org/9781108984355

DOI: 10.1017/9781108988377

First published 2023

A catalogue record for this publication is available from the British Library.

ISBN 978-1-108-98435-5 Paperback
ISSN 2632-0746 (online)
ISSN 2632-0738 (print)

Beckett and Stein

Elements in Beckett Studies

DOI: 10.1017/9781108988377
First published online: May 2023

Georgina Nugent
University of Vienna

Abstract: What motivated Beckett, in 1937, to distance himself from the 'most recent work' of his mentor James Joyce and instead praise the writings of Gertrude Stein as better reflecting his 'very desirable literature of the non-word'? This Element conducts the first extended comparative study of Stein's role in the development of Beckett's aesthetics. In doing so it redresses the major critical lacuna that is Stein's role and influence on Beckett's nascent bilingual aesthetics of the late 1930s. It argues for Stein's influence on the aesthetics of language Beckett developed throughout the 1930s, and on the overall evolution of his bilingual English writings, contending that Stein's writing was itself inherently bilingual. It forwards the technique of renarration – a form of repetition identifiable in the work of both authors – as a deliberate narrative strategy adopted by both authors to actualise the desired semantic tearing concordant with their aesthetic praxes in English.

Keywords: Samuel Beckett, Gertrude Stein, influence, repetition, bilingualism

ISBNs: 9781108984355 (PB), 9781108988377 (OC)
ISSNs: 2632-0746 (online), 2632-0738 (print)

Contents

1 Introduction: 'Grammar Is in Our Power'[1]

Samuel Beckett's letter to Axel Kaun, dated 9 July 1937, has become a key reference point in critical studies and accounts of Beckett 'The Esthetic Explorer', as Ruby Cohn classifies him in her introduction to *Disjecta* (2001, 11). While the critical importance of Beckett's expressed desire to tear at language has long been acknowledged as an indication of his evolving aesthetics of language, critics have tended to neglect the fact that Beckett specified he wished to do so in a manner akin to what Gertrude Stein had already achieved. I quote from the relevant passage in the letter to Kaun:

> It is indeed getting more and more difficult, even pointless, for me to write in formal English. And more and more my language appears to me like a veil which one has to tear apart in order to get to those things (or the nothingness) lying behind it. Grammar and style! To me they seem to have become [...] irrelevant. [...] Since we cannot dismiss it all at once, at least we do not want to leave anything undone that may contribute to its disrepute. To drill one hole after another into it until that which lurks behind, be it something or nothing, starts seeping through – I cannot imagine a higher goal for today's writer. [...] At first, it can only be a matter of somehow inventing a method of verbally demonstrating this scornful attitude vis-a-vis the word. [...]
>
> Perhaps Gertrude Stein's Logographs come closer to what I mean. The fabric of the language has at least become porous, if regrettably only quite by accident and as a consequence of a procedure somewhat akin to the technique of Feininger. The unhappy lady (is she still alive?) is undoubtedly still in love with her vehicle, if only, as a mathematician is with his numbers; for him the solution of the problem is of very secondary interest, yes, as the death of numbers, it must seem to him indeed dreadful. (Beckett, 2009c, 518–19)

This excerpt indicates that, by 1937, Beckett had encountered enough of Stein's writing to form a definite opinion of this specific aspect of her oeuvre. Beckett's interest in her 'logographs', a comment that not only suggests he had in mind a work such as *Tender Buttons* – published in its entirety in issue fourteen of Eugène Jolas's *transition* (1928) – but also indicates, by means of its very specificity, that Stein's work also contained non-logographic writing.[2] Stein's appearance in this letter suggests that, dissatisfied with the latest work by James Joyce, Beckett had begun to admire the work of an author not only removed from, but entirely at odds with, the Joyce circle. This is evinced in Beckett's choice of Stein as the artist whose aesthetics of writing (as he understood them) are close to his idea of the 'highe[st] goal for today's writer' (Beckett, 2009c, 518) – a significant statement, coming as it

---

[1] Stein, 1975, 73.

[2] For a detailed analysis of why *Tender Buttons*, and specifically Stein's publications in *transition*, represent a likely source for Beckett's reading of Stein, see Nugent-Folan (2013).

does in July 1937, less than two years before the publication of Joyce's *Finnegans Wake*.

To a degree this U-turn is understandable: this was, after all, a period in Beckett's development when he was attempting to, as Mark Nixon puts it, 'get away from Joyce' (2011, 2). An engagement with a figure as anathematic to Joyce as Stein makes sense, for within the confines of the Parisian Left Bank, the Joyce and Stein coteries were the veritable north and south poles of European English-language modernism as it stood throughout the 1920s and 1930s. To defect from one to the other (even in the gestural manner affected within this letter) was a significant act of defiance, both in terms of coterie allegiance and, more importantly, in terms of the major differences that existed between Joyce and Stein's aesthetics of language. And while this irreverence is wholly in line with the iconoclastic Beckett of the 1930s, at the same time Beckett's identification with Stein's work is, admittedly, a guarded one. He appears not to know if Stein is alive or dead – Stein died in 1946 – and refers to her as an 'unhappy lady' whose innovative use of language was developed 'regrettably only quite by accident' (Beckett, 2009c, 519).

Depending on how you interpret Beckett's description of Stein as an 'unglückliche Dame' (Beckett, 2009c, 515) – Martin Esslin translates this as 'unfortunate lady' (Beckett, 2001, 53), whereas Viola Westbrook presents Stein as an 'unhappy lady' (Beckett, 2009c, 519) – Beckett's portrait testifies to the influence of the zealous anti-Stein sentiments propounded by the Joyce circle in Paris on his opinion of her character – Stein was very much persona non grata for anyone who wished to maintain a friendly association with Joyce. But beyond this, Beckett was careful to avoid making too strong a connection between his own aesthetic and the work of Stein for other, more personal reasons: for a writer who, in 1931, apologised to Charles Prentice for the 'stink' of Joyce in 'Sedendo et Quiescendo' and wrote of his desire to 'endow' his work with his 'own odours' (Beckett, 2009c, 81), such a connection risked merely replacing the 'stink' of Joyce (a scent he was actively working to deodorise) with that of Stein. Nevertheless, this excerpt indicates that Stein's capacity to underscore the grammars of the English language had caught Beckett's attention by 1937. Further still, Stein's work was closer to Beckett's proposed 'literature of the non-word' than 'the most recent work of Joyce' which has, Beckett notes, 'nothing at all to do with such a programme' (2009c, 519) – a major declaration for a writer on the cusp of realising the aesthetics of language he had been working towards for more than a decade.

To see Beckett distinguish his aesthetics from the work of Joyce, as he does in the Kaun letter, and instead situate his preferred aesthetics as closer to the work of Stein can and has been read through the lens of the conflicting coteries of the

Stein and Joyce circles on the Parisian Left Bank. This is a major factor as to why Beckett scholars have largely neglected the Stein connection. The connection with Joyce is just too easy, too well established and too well documented to ignore. Similarly, the assertion of a Stein connection is – given the extent of the animosity between the Joyce and Stein circles – a steadfastly off-limits prospect, one made all the more difficult by the distinct lack of reading traces in relation to Beckett's encounters with Stein's work. Remarking on the 'relativity of the material traces of his reading' that are discernible in Beckett's library, Dirk Van Hulle and Nixon acknowledge the inherent limits and dangers of relying solely on extant material: 'what is still present is evidently useful, as long as it does not blind us to the numerous intertexts that have left no trace' (2013, 53). Tracing influence in the form of comparability of style or technical approaches towards the realisation of aesthetic aims – which is what this Element intends to do – is an approach that is distinct from studies that discern influence through intertext. Van Hulle and Nixon's caution is therefore important to bear in mind when it comes to considering the role Stein played in Beckett's developing aesthetics: this is not an influence that can be readily mapped through material traces.

Yet despite Beckett's own reticence, and despite the relative sparsity of material traces of his engagement with Stein's work, their names have cropped up in tandem in scholarly studies of the modernist period. As early as 1981 Marjorie Perloff acknowledges the stylistic comparability of their writings by situating them within the same strand of modernist poetics. Perloff identifies a thread of dissatisfaction with received language and linguistic representation running through the works of Beckett, Stein, Ezra Pound, Arthur Rimbaud and William Carlos Williams. In doing so, she situates Beckett in an alternative strand of modernist aesthetics to that of Joyce. Yet, while Perloff places Beckett and Stein within the same strand of modernist poetics, when she briefly examines their work together she settles on a somewhat tenuous point of stylistic dissimilarity, not stylistic proximity (1999, 206). In her introduction to *Disjecta*, Cohn also gestures towards a comparability between the two by referring to the Stein connection as one that *might have been* (Cohn, 2001, 11), and indeed it is this very *might*, its limits, its technical and stylistic manifestations, that is the focus of this Element. James Knowlson also comes close to claiming a definite connection between the two when, in *Images of Beckett*, he states that in transitioning to writing in French Beckett was *perhaps* hoping to achieve something along the lines of Stein's logographs (2003, 37). Again, the purpose of this Element is to explore the limits of this *might have been*, this *perhaps* connection, to examine how it may have been realised pragmatically in their work.

More recently, the Beckett-Stein connection has begun to receive renewed attention and this Element builds on this emergent and increasingly dynamic field of interest within Beckett studies by exploring Stein's role in Beckett's evolving aesthetic praxis throughout the 1930s and the emergence of his bilingual oeuvre.[3] It posits Stein as a figure both suitable for and deserving of consideration as one of Beckett's most prominently discernible contemporaneous literary influences, and situates Stein as a key figure not only in the evolution of Beckett's aesthetics as articulated in the Kaun letter of 1937 but also in his transition from a 'monolingual polyglot' whose work showed definite stylistic assonances with that of Joyce to a 'bilingual Anglophone' writer, a transition that ultimately facilitated his evolution into a 'bilingual Francophone' author and self-translator.[4]

Repetition is one of the most obvious points of convergence between Beckett and Stein, and one that has received some critical attention, notably in the form of Bruce Kawin's chapter-length comparative study of Beckett and Stein's engagement with repetition (1972, 131–45). Steven Connor cites Kawin extensively in his study *Samuel Beckett: Repetition, Theory, Text* (1988), which itself can be considered the most prominent study of repetition in relation to Beckett. According to Connor the 'proliferation of minima' (1988, 14) in Beckettian repetition resembles the superabundance of Joyce or Proust. The third, unmentioned and more suitable figure here is Stein; indeed, to appropriate Connor's term, Stein's prose style in *The Making of Americans* could be classified as a *superabundance* of minima. Beckett's adoption of the minimal in the form of simple word forms of the kind absent from his verbose early writings – what Banfield refers to as the 'nonproductive modifiers' (2003, 15) and what Porter Abbott (borrowing heavily from Banfield) classifies as 'nonproductive words' (2010, 213) – marks a turning point in his aesthetic development. Rather than declaring Beckett's proliferation of minima as resembling the work of Proust or Joyce then, instead, it distinguishes him from them.

This 'proliferation of minima' (Connor, 1988, 14) emerges as a major point of stylistic divergence between Beckett and Joyce. Carrying the analogy further, it also distinguishes the stylistic and aesthetic praxes of Stein and Joyce, with

---

[3] See, for example, Abbott (2010), Carville (2018), Nguyen (2013), Nugent-Folan (2013, 2015, 2022), Powell (2018).

[4] These three terms are direct translations of Chiara Montini's typology for Beckett's career as a bilingual writer in her study *'La bataille du soliloque': Genèse de la poétique bilingue de Samuel Beckett (1929–1946)* (2007). Montini outlines three major phases in the evolution of Beckett bilingualism: 'Le monolinguisme polyglotte', 'Le bilinguisme anglophone' and 'Le bilinguisme francophone' (2007, 20, 95, 177). I translate these as 'monolingual polyglot', 'bilingual Anglophone' and 'bilingual Francophone', respectively, and will make use of Montini's typology throughout this Element.

Stein's superabundantly minimal language standing in diametric opposition to the Joycean 'apotheosis of the word' (Beckett, 2009c, 519). The proximate nature of these assessments of Beckett and Stein's interest in minima and repetition is a further indication of the potential for a lucrative aesthetic connection to be made between their respective stylistic praxes, particularly when it comes to word form repetitions. With a view to teasing out Stein's role in Beckett's transition towards a bilingual writing praxis, this Element focusses on the lexical and syntactic aspects of the so-called bilingual turn that occurred in Beckett's writings from roughly 1937 on, with a specific interest in how this was first effected in the English language and in prioritising a language-focussed methodology that exposes Stein's writings to direct and pragmatic comparatives with Beckett's own. After all, if we are to conduct a study of what it was about Stein's writing that gave Beckett the impression that the fabric of language was being rendered porous, it is important to avoid, wherever possible, recourse to the very metaphors Beckett employs to articulate his vision of a 'literature of the non-word' (2009c, 520).[5] In tracing and comparing the trajectory of both authors' engagements with linguistic representation in English, I propose that Beckett and Stein adopted an identical stylistic technique combining repetition and a grammar-led adaptation of the repetitious act that I define as renarration.[6]

Renarration is a development of the technique of denarration introduced by Brian Richardson in his essay 'Denarration in Fiction: Erasing the Story in Beckett and Others' (2001), later developed by Van Hulle (2014) and Juliet Taylor-Batty, who employs a slightly different term, '*décomposition*' ['decomposition'] (2013, 146–79; emphasis in original), that nevertheless signifies the same technique. Both terms – denarration and *décomposition* – ultimately refer to the same technical praxis of 'narrative negation' (Richardson, 2001, 168) wherein an initial statement is redacted, with Van Hulle noting that this negation may occur on a varying scale or 'continuum rang[ing] from denarration "light" to substantial narrative negations as forms of "extreme narrations"' (2014, 26).

---

[5] Specifically 'Literatur des Unworts' (Beckett, 2009c, 515). A precise translation of this German neologism is difficult. Viola Westbrook translates this phrase as 'literature of the non-word' (520), whereas Martin Esslin translates it as 'literature of the unword' (Beckett, 2001, 173). For convenience, I adopt Westbrook's translation, as in her rendering of 'des Unworts' as 'non-word' she arguably allows for the coining of neologisms that, technically speaking, are complete word units but nevertheless make little semantic sense. Thus, a word does not effectively function as a word because it inhibits the relaying of semantic certitude (Beckett, 2009c, 515, 520).

[6] This term has seen previous use in the area of contemporary performance theory, specifically in relation to what David Shirley and Jane Turner classify as 'themes related to a sense of *loss* or *trauma* as well as notions of *blankness*, *presence*, *embodiment*, and *fracture*' (2013, ii–iii; emphasis in original). This Element deviates from this interpretation and instead defines renarration in a strictly literal sense as repeated passages of text that are accompanied by grammatical modifications.

Such an epanorthotically tinged narrative procedure, as Taylor-Batty notes, results in passages that are 'stylistically [...] orderly, rhythmical and grammatically correct; [yet,] semantically [...] confusing' (2013, 173). But the vast majority of Beckett's repeated passages do not abide by this twofold strategy of assertion/negation of assertion. Nor is the narrative strategy in these repetitions solely confined to that of negation.

Situating denarration within a wider context of revisionary narratological techniques, one that is not tied to a two-step process of action and redaction and instead consists of something more along the lines of (i) assertion, reassertion and *re*-reassertion, or (ii) assertion, redaction and reassertion, brings us to the field of reference encompassed by the technique of renarration. Its scope is significantly wider, often extending far beyond the twofold strategy of denarration, and can take the following formats:

(i) Using a term's semantic content against itself through immediate and recurrent single-word repetitions that serve to undo or undermine the term's heretofore definitive meaning.

(ii) Manipulating the syntax of the sentence through the use of other grammatical modifiers in tandem with repetitions so as to enforce oppositional or incompatible semantics and incite a term to suggest its own asymptote, or to sabotage its capacity to securely signify anything at all.

With these points in mind, consider the following examples – they intimate a variant strategy to the examples of denarration as defined by Richardson, one that is revisionary in its intent as opposed to being explicitly concerned with denarration:

> Mrs. Edwards who is Mrs. Taylor but Mr. Taylor is not Mr. Taylor. Literalness is not deceptive it destroys similarity (Stein, 1975, 70)

> Walter a grammar repeat a name and call it Danny that is if he was called Sarah Amelia and there was callousness. Start again (56)

> the same shining very colored [*sic*] rid of no round color (Stein, 2014, 22)

In these examples Stein deviates from the straightforward assertion and redaction of denarration to a more complex retreat involving a successive series of revisions and re-revisions to her initial statement. Stein's statement from *How To Write*, just quoted, that 'Literalness is not deceptive it destroys similarity' (1975, 70) is particularly pertinent to the technique of renarration in that literal renarration serves to 'destroy' the terms' capacity to signify the otherwise usually semantically nuanced items they signify.

Both Stein and Beckett engender a systematic praxis of renarration throughout their writings, and this Element will focus on how these renarrative techniques facilitated the strategic manipulation of the syntax of the English language, enabling them to induce what Beckett metaphorically refers to in his letter to Kaun as a 'tearing' at 'the fabric of the language' (Beckett, 2009c, 519). Both authors employed renarration as a strategy of semantic and syntactic tearing that enabled them to pragmatically interfere with the meaning-making capacity of language through the manipulation of the sinews of language itself. In short, renarration facilitates the torn, membranous vision of language as a 'literature of the non-word' Beckett calls for in the letter to Kaun (520).

This Element argues that renarration was a conscious strategy adopted and developed by both authors, and that it was a particular feature of Stein's writing of which Beckett took note. This again is crucial if we are to consider Stein as a valid and viable influence on the development of Beckett's aesthetics as they stood in the 1930s, with Stein's writing, from the perspective of technic and style, enriching his understanding of how to undermine the 'Grammar and style!' of the English language (Beckett, 2009c, 519). Again, Stein's reputation as an esoteric writer, together of course with the somewhat disparaging context within which Beckett mentions her in the context of the letter, has hampered a pragmatic assessment of how Steinian 'word-storming' (520) may have fed Beckett's understanding of the technical machinations through which one can undermine the English language.

The following five sections work to conclusively demonstrate Stein's relevance as an aesthetic model to Beckett throughout the mid-to-late 1930s and thereafter.[7] Section 2 examines Beckett and Stein's respective non-fiction writings on language in order to establish the grounds for making an assured connection between Beckett's attitude towards language as expressed in 1937

---

[7] Given the confines of the Element form, this Element's generic scope and textual corpus is necessarily limited. With respect to genre, I focus on Beckett and Stein's fictional and non-fictional output, to the exclusion of their respective engagements with the genres of theatre and poetry: this is a topic for a further study. Although Stein's work had been translated in periodicals as early as 1928's *Anthologie de la nouvelle poésie américaine* (ed. Eugène Jolas), and in book form with the publication of *Morceaux choisis de la fabrication des américains* in 1929, Stein's first published book-length composition in French did not appear until *Picasso* (1938). Stein wrote and published almost exclusively in English (Wilson, 1974, 39, 146, 148), with the exception of *Picasso* (translated into English by Stein's partner Alice Toklas). Because of this, a comparative study of their writings in or between French is inappropriate within the particular confines of this Element. The corpus of Stein texts is confined to a selection of her writings in English that were published in book or serial form during her lifetime, specifically in the years that preceded Beckett's reference to her work in the Kaun letter of 1937 – that is, texts Beckett may himself have had the opportunity to read. In the case of Beckett, the focus is confined to Beckett's non-fiction writings and his nascent bilingual anglophone works written in the aftermath of the letter (specifically, the text of *Watt*), together with the English versions of a number of his later bilingual francophone writings (namely *Texts for Nothing*, *How It Is* and the *Nohow On* texts). The absence of references to other texts from Beckett's oeuvre should thus not be considered an indication of an absence of comparable material.

and Stein's own mature, and – by the 1930s – well-deliberated aesthetics of language. The texts covered represent Beckett and Stein's most pointed attempts at articulating their frustrations with received language, their respective aesthetics of language and their efforts at realising these aesthetics. Section 3 compares Beckett and Stein's respective renarrative praxes by reading Beckett's *Watt*, a text Shane Weller classifies as 'a decidedly transitional work' (2021, 22), alongside Stein's magnum opus, *The Making of Americans: Being a History of a Family's Progress*. These two texts are both unique in each author's oeuvre and yet they will be shown to have remarkable similarities. Both display examples of unique English-language idiolects and enact deliberate violations against the English language in the form of repetitions and permutations that defy and defer the capacity to derive normative semantic or syntactic sense from language or narrative. Section 4 focusses on the role of grammatical modifiers in iterations that, in line with Beckett's pronouncement in the Kaun letter, are significantly more 'efficient' (Beckett, 2009c, 518), in the form of renarrations involving verbs, nouns or pronouns. While grammatical modifiers, by definition, delimit and make specific the semantic remit of the term against which they are attached, both Beckett and Stein frequently tend to do the opposite, making language and these delimited terms appear less certain, less specific and less distinct. These smaller-scale repetitions employ grammar modifiers to interrogate the subjects of their individual sentences on a more discrete, stylistically nuanced and – arguably – more effective level than the lumbering repetitious meanderings found throughout *Watt* and *The Making of Americans*.

Just as Beckett himself developed a method of writing bilingually in English, Stein similarly constructed a versatile, syntactically complex and semantically esoteric oeuvre while writing in an exclusively anglophone dialect, a mode of writing that may be termed 'multi-dialectical writing'. The development of Beckett's bilingual English throughout *Watt* is therefore directly analogous with aspects of Stein's own writings in, through and against the English language, as will be explored throughout Section 5. Section 6 delineates the comparability between Beckett's aesthetics of failure and what we might term Stein's aesthetics of de-creation so as to make explicit the remarkable proximity between Beckett's so-called fidelity to failure (2001, 145) and Stein's similar pursuit of error and the inexact throughout her writings. Taken together, this Element works to both introduce and make clear the significance of Stein's role in Beckett's aesthetic development: her writings facilitated the development of Beckett's bilingual English writing style, ultimately allowing him to not only transition away from the monolingual polyglottism that permeated his early writings, but to successfully evolve his aesthetic praxis so that it was no longer as inhibited by the English 'Grammar and style!' (Beckett, 2009c, 518) that was posing him such difficulty at the time of his letter to Kaun in 1937, when he would cite Stein as a reference point or waymark on his journey.

2 Grammar Bound: Writings on Language

This is a sentence. [. . .] It is a sentence (Stein, 1975, 197)

Prior to 1937 both Beckett and Stein's attentions were largely confined to the English language.[8] Beckett's expressions of dissatisfaction with English in 1937 occurred during a period of creative stasis; a period spent, by his own summation, 'doing nothing' (Beckett, 2009c, 520). In the late 1930s, with few publications to his name and what Nixon describes as a 'desperate need to be published' (2007, 217), Beckett was accompanied by hard-to-lose social and aesthetic connections with Joyce, and a corresponding urge to establish stylistic difference between himself and his mentor. His non-fiction writing from this period seems largely to consist of complaints against established or fellow emerging authors, without really articulating in these diatribes how he would go about doing things differently. Seán Kennedy nicely captures this contra-indicative situation with the phrase 'iconoclasts need their icons' (2011, 59). Kennedy is speaking here of Beckett's engagement with the Irish literary scene between the years 1929 and 1956, but this willingness to 'usefully complicat[e] any reading of Beckett as merely aloof from Irish affairs' (59) can be extended to Beckett's engagement with authors on mainland Europe too, and indeed more generally to the mammoth hold English 'Grammar and style!' (Beckett, 2009c, 518) was exerting on his capacity to write in the latter half of the 1930s.

Stein declares herself similarly 'miserable' (1975, 30) in 1931 and includes words that indicate personal disillusionment, frustration, difference and self-doubt over whether a written item is 'correct'. 'Is that a possible tense' (106), Stein writes, some twenty-two years after her first book-length publication in English – 1909's *Three Lives*. In contrast to Beckett, these expressions of dissatisfaction occur during a particularly active and financially rewarding period in her writing life, a time when she was on the cusp of achieving mass recognition and a certain renown in the public sphere, albeit for *The Autobiography of Alice B. Toklas*, as opposed to her more difficult writings. Beyond the *Lectures in America* (1935), which were composed to be delivered orally and to a largely non-specialist crowd, Stein's

---

[8] Although Stein's work had been translated into French on her behalf in periodicals as early as 1928, Stein's first written and published book-length composition in French did not appear until 1938's *Picasso* (Wilson, 1974, 148, 146, 39). In the case of Beckett, as Stephen Stacey notes, prior to his permanent relocation to Paris in 1937, 'English – albeit an increasingly idiosyncratic form of English – had up to that point been his preferred language for literary prose' (2013).

How to Write, published three years earlier in 1931, contains perhaps her most engaged analysis of language. In *How to Write*, Stein's focus is on the grammatical components of language – nouns, pronouns, adjectives, verb, adverbs and punctuation. As the title suggests, Stein is largely concerned with how to engage in the act of writing, but the text has broader concerns, being in fact an almost forensic analysis of how language operates. Using the voice of a fictional Alice B. Toklas in 1933's *The Autobiography of Alice B. Toklas*, Stein refers to it as her 'treatises on grammar, sentences, paragraphs, vocabulary etcetera' (2001, 226).

Stein promotes herself throughout these publications and lectures from the early 1930s as a theorist of language and of atypical grammars in particular, a topic Beckett never broached as publicly or in as much detail. Stein's role as a theoretician of grammar – as a 'grammarian' (Stein, 1975, 109) – is important, as her theories were largely self-reflexive, referring back to and elucidating her own writings. Throughout these lectures and essays Stein is relentless in her interrogations of the English language, and specifically whether the words she has used – correct or incorrect – really capture what she is trying to communicate. All can be considered indicative of Stein's innate suspiciousness regarding the filaments of language.

How to Write contains a multitude of direct engagements with the materiality of the English language in the form of direct references to grammar. This comes in the form of straightforward statements such as 'This is a sentence. [...] It is a sentence' (1975, 197), a meta-commentary on the restrictive and thus sentence-like structure of a sentence. Stein includes sentences that list the constituent parts of sentences – 'A sentence is made of an article a verb and a noun' (155) – and even creates sentences out of lists of grammatical terms alone, following these lists with simple interrogatives of the terms she has just listed:

> Adverb adjective and noun.
> Verb adjective and noun.
> Participle adverb and noun.
> Participle adverb verb adverb and noun.
> What is a participle verb adverb and noun. (1975, 118)

Such a listing of 'sentences', composed of the nominal terms for the grammatical particulars of sentences, is a conscious attempt at making her reader hyper-aware of the grammars at work within any given sentence. Stein exposes the fundamental conflict between the names of the terms and the items these terms themselves signify when taken for their lexical value alone. The 'Grammar and style!' of the sentence, the very 'fabric of the language' (Beckett, 2009c, 519), is always on show in this exposed, almost brutalist approach to demonstrating how materially dependant – or, as Beckett puts it, how 'arbitrary' (518) – these terms are unless invested with a certain meaning.

Beckett similarly exploits units of grammar. The narrator/narrated in *How It Is* observes the functional title given to terms as they operate within the 'natural order' (Cordingley, 2007, 185) of a sentence unit, showing an acute awareness of the changes that occur within a sentence as the sentence progresses: 'sudden series subject object subject object quick succession and away' (Beckett, 2009b, 7). This sentence reads as a literal description of the material happenings of the clausal unit, but one that sacrifices the body of the narrative to instead focus on the clausal unit *as a narrative*. The narrator of 'Text for Nothing VI' comments on whether nouns are singular or plural (Beckett, 2009e, 27), while in 'Text for Nothing II' the narrator not only observes that 'superlatives have lost their charm' (9), but displays a keen awareness of the movement of grammatical units within a sentence as the sentence transitions from beginning to end: 'The words too, slow, slow, the subject dies before it comes to the verb, words are stopping too' (9). Similar instances of narrative self-awareness occur elsewhere, from the 'plethoric reflexive pronoun' mentioned in *Watt* (2009f, 4n1) to repeated meta-commentary on the verb tenses used during specific sentences in *Texts for Nothing* and *How It Is*: 'No no, I'll speak not of the future, I'll speak in the future' (2009e, 12); 'a little less of to be present past future and conditional of to be and not to be' (2009b, 31). An almost identical process occurs in *How to Write*, with Stein listing the grammar functions *as they function* within the sentence: 'Begin a participle by their stretches. Transitive and intransitive aid obeyed with joy. [. . .] The complement in grammar' (1975, 119).

Both authors frequently use the appearance of specific modifiers as an opportunity to break the narrative contract and point out specifics of grammar to the reader. As noted previously, specific verb tenses (such as the 'plethoric reflexive pronoun' (2009f, 4n1) of *Watt*) or changes in verb tense have all been employed by either author in passages containing a direct address to the reader or sections that acknowledge the act of narration in a metanarrative process. This shared tendency towards irony, metanarratives and wilful self-contradiction when it comes to their engagements with punctuation and the particulars of orthography can be linked to their respective attempts at highlighting the de-mimetic potential of language, that is to say, of its capacity to distort, to misrepresent and to render things 'ill seen ill said' (2009a, 72) and 'missaid' (81). Beyond verb and verb tense, punctuation in particular comes under repeated scrutiny, as in the following examples:

> And so I almost never use a comma. The longer, the more. [. . .] (Stein, 1998, 321); I always found it [the question mark] positively revolting. (316–17); How hideous is the semi colon. I say an external agency; for of my own volition (Beckett, 2009f, 135); just enough to speak enough to hear not even comma a mouth an ear (Beckett, 2009b, 68); here a parenthesis (56)

These overt references to punctuation are employed as a further means of instilling their texts with the 'nominalistic irony' Beckett begrudgingly acknowledges as a necessary element in 1937 (2009d, 520). Moreover, both Beckett and Stein take this further, manipulating actual punctuation marks throughout their writings in a form of *non*-nominalistic irony that enables them to instil syntactic atypicality or dissonance throughout their texts. For example, Stein displays an extreme aversion to the appearance of certain punctuations in her prose from *The Making of Americans* onwards, with a particular dislike of question marks, exclamation points, quotation marks and commas, which she variously labels as 'the completely most uninteresting [. . .] positively revolting [. . .] unnecessary, [. . .] ugly [. . .] things in punctuation' (Stein, 1998, 316–17). Stein's aversion to the comma is resolutely manifest throughout *How to Write*, a text that contains no commas and is thus comparable to Beckett's *How It Is*; a text that, while extreme in its lack of punctuative entities, corresponds to an overall lessening of punctuation throughout Beckett's later writings.

Such actions return attention to the process of writing and the materiality of the text, with the act of representing in language continually highlighted as an artificial and perpetually inaccurate process. By presenting the events in an excessively literal and self-reflexive manner, drawing frequent attention to orthographic features of the text, they implicitly query the events that would have been expunged from a more grammatically correct or narratively acceptable version. The sentence is presented less as something that necessarily has to make semantic sense and more as a 'proposition' that is, as the *OED* definition of 'sentence' states, made in 'an artificial [. . .] language', making sense only within a very small range and subject to change or a revision of terms at any moment. Beckett and Stein's respective engagement with language at the level of its fabric thus indicates a shared and acute awareness of the material facets of language, together with a willingness to engage with their medium on a visceral (and consequently both literal *and* material) level.

This is perhaps one of the most straightforward connections between Beckett and Stein, with both authors spending a considerable amount of time remonstrating against the inefficacies of the English language. Their dissatisfaction with standard English manifests most obviously in the form of straightforward expressions of the same, specifically regarding how nouns, pronouns and other key grammatical units contained within the bodies of sentences impacts their attempts at capturing or relaying events through language. While Beckett declared the grammars and style of formal English 'irrelevant' (2009c, 518) in 1937, in 1931 Stein was referring to writing as a task that was discouraging and to sentences as items that caused her distress or made her miserable:

'Discouragement looks like it'; 'I am very miserable about sentences. I can cry about sentences'; 'Sentences make one sigh' (1975, 19, 30, 32). If Beckett felt encased by 'Grammar and style!' (2009c, 518), Stein declared herself (or rather, the English language) 'grammar bound' (1975, 65), with the grammars of the language restricting what can be said. To be 'grammar bound' presents grammar and, by extension, language as a 'sentence'. It implies that the language user is tied to the structural aspects of language, that they act as a sort of inhibitor to a freer mode of expression. Stein plays on the dual meaning of the term 'sentence' throughout the entirety of *How to Write*. In doing so she acknowledges the limiting nature of the linguistic medium, continually drawing attention to what Beckett, in his letter to Kaun, refers to as 'that terrifyingly arbitrary material of the word surface' (2009c, 519).

Just as Beckett observes in 'Recent Irish Poetry' that 'the new thing that has happened' is in fact 'the old thing that has happened again, namely the breakdown of the object' (Beckett, 2001, 70), Stein also observes that this same crisis of the word is cyclical. In her lecture 'What Is English Literature' she elaborates on her theory that throughout the history of the English language, several such periods of crisis and revolution have taken place (Stein, 1998, 195–223). In stark contrast to these previous periods of nominal inebriation and immediacy where the noun was truly present as 'the name in origin' (1975, 145), the modern(ist) era, Stein argues, is characterised by a state of crisis wherein the connection between word and object is disputed. Rather than experience events in their immediacy, these core nominal forms are, as she puts it in the following description from *Tender Buttons*, 'imitation[s], more imitation[s], imitations succeed imitations' (2014, 42). Stein displays an acute understanding of this problem of representation, classified elsewhere by Beckett as 'apperception' (2001, 70), although she herself presents the issue as inherently ontological: 'One cannot come back too often to the question what is knowledge and to the answer knowledge is what one knows' (Stein, 1998, 195). Her attempts to disable and subvert the apperceptive process is epitomised in her justification of the famous, but often mocked phrase 'rose is a rose is a rose is a rose' (1993, 187):

> Can't you see that when language was new – as it was with Chaucer and Homer – the poet could use the name of a thing and the thing was really there. [...] And can't you see that after hundreds of years had gone by and thousands of poems had been written, he could call on those words and find that they were just wornout [*sic*] literary words. (2004, 7)

Stein refers to linguistic signs as dead items, a 'specimen' that once held an innate capacity to captivate in terms of their ability to convey an object, image, or expression: 'A sign is the specimen spoken' (2014, 42). Similarly, throughout

Beckett's fictions, older words, or rather, the same words when expressed in an earlier temporal period, are considered to have had a more immediate or vivid meaning when they were expressed *then* as opposed to when they are expressed *now*. In *How It Is* the narrator/narrated implies that older versions of white were whiter, older blues were bluer, and older dusts were dustier: 'the white there was then'; 'the dust there was then'; 'the blue there was then' (Beckett, 2009b, 37, 37, 61). Both *How It Is* and *Texts for Nothing* contain further references to 'old words' and 'ancient scraps' (2009b, 34, 116), to 'old stories', 'old questions and answers' and 'old thing[s]' (2009e, 5, 29).

Beckett and Stein also appear suspicious of the naturalness of this so-called natural order (Beckett, 2009b, 14) of language, making a distinction between the natural in terms of the learned, and the natural in terms of reality and lived experience. Acknowledging that 'there are different ways of making of, of course' (Stein, 1975, 134), Stein not only queries the primacy of received language but rather, much like the character of Pim in Beckett's *How It Is*, she openly challenges the idea that the learnt or received is the 'natural order more or less' (Beckett, 2009b, 14). This querying of the primacy of the 'natural order' wherein the 'natural' is a pre-established and pre-approved 'definitive' word is much the same complaint Beckett fields in 'Recent Irish Poetry' when he bemoans the perceived nullity of 'celebrat[ing] the cold comforts of apperception' (Beckett, 2001, 70). These excerpts indicate that Stein could easily have been included among the group of (exclusively male) artists Beckett praised in 1934's 'Recent Irish Poetry' for their awareness of what he classifies as a 'rupture of the lines of communication' (70).

In her fictional writings of the 1910s and 1920s Stein actively sought out alternate forms of expression so as to avoid the recourse to 'apperception' (Beckett, 2001, 70). 'Why write in nouns?' Stein asks (1998, 313). Instead of putting up with stale nominal structures, why not attempt to rename them, as she attempted to do in *Tender Buttons*, to 'mak[e] it be a thing that could be named without using its name' (330). While the resultant text may not have fully actualised Stein's aesthetic aspirations, the impetus that led her to attempt to find other words to apply to existent words, and to deem certain items unsatisfactorily named, points to a larger dissatisfaction with language systems that places her assessment of the English language in direct complement with Beckett's.

The requisites of grammatically correct sentences exert their authority over language and language users such that they begin to 'think in sentences' (Stein, 1975, 149) and either experience dissatisfaction with their output, as Beckett did, or operate through 'apperception' (Beckett, 2001, 70) as Beckett did not wish to do. Stein makes a similar criticism of the tendency to rely on apperception in her observation that 'If you think in sentences you are not easily pleased' (Stein, 1975, 149). It is easier to 'think in grammar' (61), Stein writes, or to 'think in sentences' – that is, to think in a corrective manner that sees 'words come before the mind [. . .] [t]his makes instant grammar' (149, 66). This sees the language user confine their thoughts and potential lexicon to a closed system of words delimited by others, to 'thinking as they thought' as Stein vividly describes it: 'Thinking in words. [. . .] Thinking as they thought' (142). These exchanges require less effort and involvement on the part of the observer, with the individual subsuming the grammars of the majority for the sake of facility: 'Successions of words are so agreeable'; 'Thinks in grammar. It is easier to know that a vocabulary can say so' (39, 61).

Rather than seeing Stein as a writer who came upon her innovations 'quite by accident' (Beckett, 2009c, 519), as Beckett contends, these excerpts posit Stein as a writer who was deeply engaged in the very same endeavours surrounding the discrediting of received language as Beckett both articulated in 1937 and later attempted to realise in his writings. Stein shared many of the unenthused if not outright dismissive attitudes towards language that Beckett articulated throughout much of his key non-fiction writings from the 1930s and thereafter. By declaring herself 'grammar bound' (Stein, 1975, 65), Stein identified an impediment to linguistic expression that was similar to the inhibiting effects of the English 'Grammar and style!' Beckett bemoans throughout his letter to Kaun (Beckett, 2009c, 518). This mutual recognition posits both artists as inhabiting a place of aesthetic similitude, or, more precisely, of aesthetic stasis wherein both are 'bound' by the grammars they are seeking to subvert or eradicate. While Beckett's exasperation is clearly evident in this letter, so too is his uncertainty regarding how to move forward with his writing. In contrast, in the case of Stein, this epithet is less a complaint or grievance and more a statement of aesthetic intent, or indeed of retrospective reflection on her life's work. Stein presents herself as an author both bound by grammar and grammar bound. By playing on the dual meaning of 'bound' – as a form of bondage or boundary and as a movement towards something – Stein acknowledges what was for her a technical approach central to her writing and one that ultimately allowed her to circumvent the limitations of her medium by manipulating the sinews and fabric of language itself so as to undermine them and render them ineffective. In other words, Stein had developed a technique of attacking language *through* language, a technique Beckett was himself looking to initiate in the period leading up to and succeeding his letter to Kaun.

By 1937 then, it can at least be claimed – the preceding passages having made this explicit – that both artists shared a comparable dissatisfaction with language, openly acknowledging the negative effect English language acquisition and the habits of language use have had on their capacity to express themselves freely. Both authors describe the grammars and learned habits of 'correct' language use as particularly difficult to avoid, and present the ingrained behaviours associated with felicitous language use as having inhibiting and restrictive effects on their writings. The strictures of 'Grammar and style!' in 'formal English' exert a modulating influence on Beckett, so much so that he speaks of a desire to be '*allowed* to violate [. . .] my own language' (2009c, 518, 520; emphasis added), feeling instead, as he did then, that he was prevented or forbidden from doing so by the rules of grammar and style.

Stein similarly presents grammar as a set of strictures that are 'indisposed' to change, prohibiting any bending of the rules: 'Grammar makes no mistakes. Grammar uses indisposes in that way' (1975, 81). Though less encumbered by English grammar than Beckett, Stein nevertheless recognised the inhibitor that was the habits of grammar and schooled language use. 'I am having it as a habit' (106), Stein writes, in a statement that is directly analogous to the habits of formal English Beckett remonstrates against. Like Beckett, Stein acknowledges that it is difficult to fully unlearn the grammars and styles of a set language: 'Grammar and resemblance could any one forget how to be told' (59). Even Stein, then, who benefitted from a far freer association with the English language than Beckett, found it difficult to unlearn the apperceptive habits of her medium: 'It is hard not to remember what it is' (32). But whereas Beckett himself was struggling at this period to come up with a method of displaying, interrogating and discrediting this facet of language, Stein was clearly aware not only of the effects of grammar in terms of its capacity to modulate and impede expression, but also that this sentiment brought on by habit was itself false – that grammar was neither infallible nor unerring; it merely relies on the user perceiving it to be so. As Stein puts it, grammar not only 'has no meaning' but 'is completely false in reflection': 'I am having it as a habit. As a habit has no meaning. I am having it as a habit. Is completely false in reflection' (106).

Both authors present language as a medium that is no longer successfully performing its communicative or representative function; it is presented as a failure, and one that both enacts sentences and perpetuates this sentencing of sentences to fail in their efforts at conveying sense. Ironically, however, both authors manage to successfully convey one key message – they are failing to communicate successfully. Language, Stein states, does not contain what is known, and it inhibits the reception of knowledge or experience so that 'nothing' is received and 'nothing' is known: 'A sentence is not what they know' (1975, 161). This is identical in sentiment to a familiar passage from *Three Dialogues* regarding 'the expression that there is nothing to express, nothing with which to express, nothing from which to express, no power to express, no desire to express, together with the obligation to express' (Beckett, 2001, 139).

Similar too is Stein's assertion that there is 'no resemblance' between the signifier and the thing itself: 'Resemblance. A grammar. There is no resemblance, it is not what they remind them to be an interval like it' (Stein, 1975, 91). Finally, Stein's forceful assertion that 'grammar is useless because there is nothing to say' (62) can be compared to Beckett's similarly minded declaration, noted earlier in this Element, that 'there is nothing to express' (Beckett, 2001, 139).

These expressions of futility regarding the act of expression are not confined to 1949's *Three Dialogues*, having earlier appeared in the form of Beckett's observation that writing in English was becoming 'pointless' (2009c, 518) in the Kaun letter of 1937. Earlier still, in a 1934 letter to Morris Sinclair, Beckett states, 'no sooner do I take up my pen to compose something in English than I get the feeling of being "de-personified"' (205). Such statements recur throughout the letters, but the fact that the latter two were themselves expressed in languages other than English (in German and French respectively) adds authenticity to these particular remarks. Similar sentiments are found throughout *Texts for Nothing*, with the narrator of 'Text for Nothing III' declaring 'all is false' while 'Text for Nothing XI' declares 'nothing is namable': 'Yes, no more denials, all is false, there is no one, it's understood, no more phrases, let us be dupes, dupes of every time and tense'; 'Name, no, nothing is namable, tell, no, nothing can be told' (Beckett, 2009e, 11, 45). Consider too the comparability of Beckett's comments with Stein's assertion that 'a sentence has no mystery. A mystery would be a reception. They receive nothing' (Stein, 1975, 34). This dissatisfaction extends beyond straightforward nominal insecurity through to the seams and sinews of lexical signifiers so that for Stein, even the pronouns are faulty: 'There is no reason why they should compare them with themselves' (125). This creates a particularly interesting point of aesthetic cohesion between the two authors, with their respective statements regarding pronominal uncertainty and insecurity at times extremely proximate: 'I do not know nor do I know if he thinks with them or without me (Stein, 1975, 19).' 'I'll be there, I won't miss it, it won't be me, I'll be here, I'll say I'm far from here, it won't be me (Beckett, 2009e, 11).'

In spite of this terminal insufficiency of language, the act of 'try[ing] to tell a story' (Beckett, 2009e, 11) or, as Stein puts it, 'telling that not telling in stories' (1975, 49) is something both authors engage in throughout their respective fictions, and it is done in spite of their prior assertions regarding the ineffectiveness of writing in language. Their situation can be paralleled with that outlined by Beckett in the third of the *Three Dialogues* in relation to Bram van Velde: ' B. – The situation is that of him who is helpless, cannot act, in the event cannot paint, since he is obliged to paint. The act is of him who, helpless, unable to act, acts, in the event paints, since he is obliged to paint' (Beckett, 2001, 145).

Elsewhere, Beckett notes in the van Velde dialogue that van Velde 'is the first to admit that to be an artist is to fail, as no other dare fail, that failure is his world' (Beckett, 2001, 145). But as has already been made clear, Stein in her writings not only tolerated the idea of failure, but actively encouraged if not pursued it throughout certain of her works, attaching the 'wrong' words to noun forms in *Tender Buttons*, for example, or creating an incomplete catalogue of peoples throughout *The Making of Americans*, defending her idiosyncratic methods with the observation that 'When I have not been right there must be something wrong' (Stein, 1995, 573).

One potential outcome of this scenario wherein their respective aesthetic credos seem to fasten on the inevitability of failure apropos linguistic representation and communication, would be to harness this terminal insufficiency and attempt to convey it. This is something both authors seem to have independently realised and, I think, sought to capitalise on – and I return to this concept in Section 6. Whether or not Stein led Beckett to this realisation is unclear and, without definitive archival evidence this uncertainty will be maintained. That said, this section has made clear that their respective articulations of dissatisfaction with the English language are strikingly similar and complementary, suggesting a strong aesthetic confluence.

Where Beckett and Stein differ in this respect can be ascribed to the evolution of their respective languages of choice. Stein's lifelong commitment to writing in English (albeit an English of her own devising) stands in counterpoint to Beckett's post-1937 extension of this practice across – and between – English and French, and the development of a bilingual compositional praxis that was, as Sam Slote puts it, 'fundamental to the workings of Beckett's texts' (2015, 205). This will be covered in greater detail in Section 5. For now it is merely important to note that whereas Stein confined herself to enacting linguistic sabotage in – and against – English, Beckett extended this practice not only *beyond* English to encompass the language of French (and later German), but *between* the English and French versions of his texts. By seeding subtle differences between the English and French versions of his works Beckett not only rendered the relationship between an 'original' work and its 'translation' problematic, but gave rise to what Slote refers to as 'a kind of linguistic atopia' wherein Beckett's texts and their translations appear 'neither French, nor English, nor Irish' (Slote, 2015, 122). This is evident in the lexical and phrasal variations Beckett introduces between translations, a feature well documented by Krance (1993, 1996), Montini (2007, 2012), Sardin (2015) and Slote (2011), and throughout the growing number of monograph outputs from the Beckett Digital Manuscript Project (Bloomsbury/UPA). It is also evident in his use of French syntactic forms that do not have ready English equivalents (as documented by Astbury, 2001), his use of what Karine Germoni and Pascale Sardin refer to as 'Beckett's deconstruction of conventional punctuation' throughout *Fin de partie* and *Endgame*, achieved 'in French with the effacement of grammatical commas, [and] in English with the calque of the French full stop' (2012, 346), and what Germoni refers to as 'la ponctuation entre deux langues [punctuation between two languages]' (2014, 283–98). While Beckett's post-1950 writings in English and French 'begin to', as Astbury notes, 'do, literally, what they please with syntax' (2001, 452), Stein confines herself to simply doing what she pleases with word forms, syntax and punctuation in English.

Though Beckett would claim then, some eight days after writing the Kaun letter, to be the only member of the 'logoclasts league', the preceding analysis makes clear that Stein's own aesthetics of language and fierce iconoclasm place her firmly in the category of premier 'logoclast' (Beckett, 2009c, 521n8), a further indication of her appropriateness as an aesthetic touchstone throughout this period in his development. In the face of such dissatisfaction, with an ill-functioning system paired with a 'fidelity to failure' (Beckett, 2001, 145) and a similarly negative appraisal of the capacity to express, both authors make a decision that is remarkable for its comparability and mutual coherency. That decision is to go on, to continue trying to narrate irrespective of the rate of failure or the unsuccessful nature of the act. 'Now I am going on. Now go on' (Stein, 1995, 664), Stein writes in 1925, some twenty-eight years before Beckett would coin a similar phrase in *L'Innomable* (1953).

3 Renarration in *The Making of Americans* and *Watt*

> What variety and at the same time what monotony, how varied it is and at the same time how, what's the word, how monotonous. What agitation and at the same time what calm, what vicissitudes within what changelessness (Beckett, 2009e, 37).

At roughly the same period in their writing careers, Beckett and Stein composed remarkably similar texts – *Watt* for Beckett and *The Making of Americans* for Stein. Both are their second completed novels, both are the longest prose works in their respective oeuvres, both are written in curious and idiosyncratic deviations on standard English containing lengthy repetitive passages, long sequences and recurrent linguistic and thematic patterns. Both *Watt* and *The Making of Americans* exhibit novel-specific idiolects that, at times, hold only a passing resemblance to standard English. Both texts can also be said to hold the theme and technique of repetition as one of the most, if not the most, prominent technical and thematic procedures present throughout. In order to demonstrate on a material level the facets explored previously, this section will isolate and study the renarration of set word forms and phrasal units relating to a core number of thematic elements readily identifiable throughout both novels in order to argue that both texts can be read as deliberate attempts at 'getting away' from formal and formalising aspects of the English language, and of the narratives construed through such formal English structures. This not only renders Beckett and Stein's aesthetics remarkably proximate. It also shows them to be repeatedly relying on and making use of the same techniques as a means of subverting the semantic and syntactic regularities of the English language.

In *The Elements of Elocution* Mark Forsyth acknowledges Stein as a particularly gifted exponent of the pleonasm, honing in on the phrase 'rose is a rose is a rose is a rose' (2013, 161), reproduced in a circular motif on Stein and Toklas's crockery, as a sort of personal insignia inscribed around the edge of their dinner plates: 'the crockery version [of the phrase 'rose is a rose is a rose is a rose'] has no beginning and no end and is therefore a case of infinite pleonasm' (161). While infinite pleonasm is technically impossible beyond typographic manipulations of the kind seen on Stein's personalised insignia, it can certainly be said to operate thematically throughout both *The Making of Americans* and *Watt*. Both texts benefit from being considered as not unsuccessful attempts at appropriating the rhetorical technique of the pleonasm (itself traditionally seen as a fault of style when used excessively) so as to bring about near-infinite pleonastic narratives.

Infinite pleonasm, or, for the purpose of accuracy, hyperextended pleonasm, is a technique both authors employ throughout *The Making of Americans* and *Watt*. In the case of *Watt* we encounter a text with near-infinite interpretative potential, a feat largely enabled by the closing line in the novel's addenda: 'no symbols where none intended' (Beckett, 2009f, 223). In the case of Stein, *The Making of Americans* appears as a text that strives for the infinite but gradually succumbs to the impossibility of this very task; or, more cynically, a text that sees its narrator gradually overcome by what Beckett in *Watt* refers to as 'fatigue and disgust' (215n1). The text begins as a history of all peoples only to be subsequently recalibrated to serve as a partial history, a history of 'them' as opposed to a history of 'all': 'there will be a history of them and now here is a beginning' (Stein, 1995, 176). Later still, in the closing passages of the novel, this recalibration is made more diminutive again by being retroactively modified to serve as a history of 'some' (925).

Aside from thematic aspirations or interpretative potentials that verge on the infinite, both texts also contain a high proportion of hyperextended pleonastic passages. The account of the Lynch family, for example, is as lengthy and permutative as some of the shorter pleonastic passages in Stein's text. Similar, albeit markedly curtailed, passages throughout *Watt* present infinite pleonasm as a thematic model around which many of the passages operate: the description of the infinite (infinite through semantic rendering, if not infinitely rendered in text) chain of figures coming and going to the Knott house in *Watt* is another example. In the case of Stein, emphasis is also placed on the fact that the Dehning and Hersland families are just two families chosen from an infinite number of 'different ones', or that particular characters focussed on throughout the text have been selected from an infinite pool. The text of *Watt* also presents Watt as part of a chain of figures similar to that from which the Dehning and Hersland families were selected, one from the many of 'all those of whom all trace is lost' (Beckett, 2009f, 51).

Despite falling short of the infinite, then, both texts adopt a thematic or systematised approach to the infinite that presents the narratives as potentially infinitesimal, as just one small aspect of larger, untold (or in Stein's case, yet to be told) narratives. To this end, their respective narrators present the narratives they recount as incomplete, imperfect, ill-arranged and inaccurately rendered. Stein makes this apparent from the onset of *The Making of Americans*, with a direct address to the reader to remind them that this 925-page account is 'perhaps' incomplete: 'yet, please reader, remember that this is perhaps not the whole of our story either' (1995, 15). Similarly, in *Watt*, the figure of Sam cautions against any tendency to view the narrative as complete by making explicit the extent to which inexactitude is infused throughout his recounting of the exchanges he has with Watt, observing that 'much fell in vain on my imperfect hearing and understanding, and much by the rushing wind was carried away, and lost forever' (Beckett, 2009f, 133), or that 'I understood as well as ever, that is to say fully one half of what won its way past my tympan' (144).

The Making of Americans can be loosely summarised, then, as one long, flawed, hypernymic repetition wherein a history of one family becomes a history of two families, and subsequently a history of *all* families. Or, as Stein puts it, a history of 'every one who ever was or is or will be living' recalibrated mid-novel into a history of 'some of them' (1995, 179; 175). Repetition, Stein argues, is the best method for spotting the nuances that constitute a given human's behaviour: 'Slowly every one in continuous repeating, to their minutest variation, comes to be clearer to some one' (284). In this opinion she is not alone, as the text of *Watt* contains similar such injunctions regarding the effect of repetition on the human person: 'For it was an attitude

become, with frequent repetition, so part of his being, that there was no more
room in his mind for resentment' (Beckett, 2009f, 25).

Stein enacts a process of continual re-specification wherein each general
category is shown to contain further subcategories, which are in turn shown to
contain *further* subcategories, thus retroactively showing themselves to be
comparatively general, and so on. Stein's interest in delineations relating to
men and women – 'Mostly they were just ordinary stupid enough women like
millions of them'; 'There are many kinds of men and there are many millions
made of each kind of them' (1995, 78, 136) – can be compared to the method
Beckett employs to detail the nuances of Watt's romantic relationship with Mrs
Gorman. This relationship is extrapolated using a similar technique to that seen
throughout Stein's narrative, with Beckett playing on the idiomatic compound
'a man's man' throughout. The text appears to specify the individual appeal (or
lack thereof) of both Watt and Mrs Gorman to the opposite and same sex, but
ends up confusing the matter further by being unable to classify them as
appealing to persons of either sex: 'Between Watt neither a man's nor
a woman's man and Mrs Gorman neither a man's nor a woman's woman?'
(Beckett, 2009f, 122). Neither Watt nor Mrs Gorman can be classified as 'a
man's man', 'a woman's man', 'a man's woman' or 'a woman's woman' (122).
The more specific the narrative is about either character's nuances, the less
specific a portrait we possess of either figure. Like Stein's Alfred Hersland they
too are 'one of a kind' (1995, 542), but we are never entirely sure what kind, or
indeed what one.

By and large, the repetitions and permutations in *Watt* proceed with an
attention to detail that is unrelentingly assiduous and accords to a relatively
closed-order system (that the final line in the 'Appendix' effectively seeks to
completely undermine). In contrast, the narrative of *The Making of Americans*
wanders between and around the utterly unquantifiable series of qualities Stein
is endeavouring to conquer through narrative collation in a way that is ill-
disciplined, forgetful, frequently illogical and often prone to randomness of
association. But it would be a mistake to consider this an accident or deficiency
of style on Stein's part. While *Watt* concludes with the trump statement 'no
symbols where none intended' (Beckett, 2009f, 223), Stein instead incorporates
this inexactness and imprecision throughout, so that each apparent progression
towards an approximation is simultaneously regressive and counterproductive.
This ultimately makes an already impossible task seem altogether less achiev-
able. At times, it is as though her narrator somehow manages to further
impossibilise the already impossible, an impossible task in itself.

Just as Beckett resolves his novel by undoing it, Stein weaves this concept of
'no symbols where none intended' (Beckett, 2009f, 223) into the very fibres of

her text throughout the course of its narration. The statement 'everybody is a real one to me, everybody is like some one else too to me' (Stein, 1995, 305) is repeated with minor variations throughout the novel, often with subtle syntactic modifications. The following three examples display further iterations of this recurrent play on 'one' as both a hypernym and hyponym, of one figure having the capacity to symbolise one, some or none:

> Mostly every one is resembling some how to some one, every one is one inside them, every one reminds some one of some other one. [. . .]
>
> Every one is themselves inside them and every one is resembling to others. [. . .]
>
> Every one is resembling somehow to some one (Stein, 1995, 332).

What begins in both texts as initial or superficial associations often gives way to much larger fields of uncertainty and mass similitude, where symbols may be apparent or not, and every 'one' may be someone or something else. The narrators' capacity to identify sameness or comparability in the face of difference becomes increasingly problematic. What may begin in either text as 'a clear resemblance' between one figure and another – or in the case of *Watt*, between one word and another – is ultimately undone by relentless renarrations that sabotage all purported comparability. As Stein puts it in the following passage, 'it began as a clear resemblance to some one, it goes on to be a confusing number of resemblances to many of them' (1995, 340).

Seven hundred pages into her novel Stein introduces a series of repetitions based on the hypernym 'family' that extends across several pages and sees her focus transition from the nuclear family to include extended relations in the form of cousins, aunts and uncles, before finally progressing to the person-specific subcategory of particular family names. These terms no longer have any generic potential and refer solely to specific persons within the Dehning and Hersland families:

> Alfred Hersland and Minnie Mason and Patrick Moore and James Flint and Mackinly Young and David Hersland and George Dehning and Hortense Dehning and Julia Hersland and Theodore Summers and William Beckling and Helen Cooke and James Cranach and Miriam Cranach and Rachel Sherman and Adolph Herman and Charles Kohler and Linder Herne and Arthur Keller and Florentine Cranach and Hilda Breslau (1995, 718–19)

Read alongside Beckett's similar account of the Lynch family in *Watt*, this excerpt from *The Making of Americans* shows itself to be remarkably proximate to Beckett's methodical delineation of the Lynch familial unit, which sees similarly lengthy and, at times, sparsely punctuated sentences containing a proliferation of figures connected by conjunctions and possessive pronouns: methodical, technical delineations of the familial unit from the general through to the hyper-specific. Though we are reminded by means of a footnote that 'the figures given here are incorrect' (Beckett, 2009f, 87), the members of Lynch family are subsequently named in detail, from 'Tom Lynch, widower, aged eighty-five years, confined to his bed with constant undiagnosed pains in the caecum' through to 'the rising generation [. . .] Sean's two little girls Roe and Cerise, [. . .] and then there were Simon's two little boys, Pat and Larry' (84–7), encompassing some four pages.

Beckett's account of the maladies of the Lynch family is infused with a series of very specific ailments, but still proceeds in a relatively uncomplicated manner through the generations. Stein's interest, in comparison, rests on a more conceptual notion of how one individual can go from healthy to ill, from alive to dead. In a further contrast with Beckett's meticulously ordered chronology, her account leaps from generation to generation without recourse to any identifiable sequence. A palpable anxiety is identifiable throughout Stein's account of the fickle nature of illness, life and death, one that includes this relatively accessible observation:

> It is natural that when there are very many of a family living and very many cousins and some aunts and uncles living that sometimes some of them should be sick ones, even that once in a while one of them should come to be a dead one. In a way it is a strange thing because very often for many years not any one in the family connection is a seriously sick one, not any one is ever thinking of any one they are then knowing as any where near to any dying. (Stein, 1995, 718)

This could serve as an apt summary of the Lynch family dilemma from Beckett's *Watt*, the members of which all suffer some form of ailment, but none of whom have yet managed to come 'any where near to any dying' (Stein, 1995, 718), until, that is, following Watt's arrival at the Knott house, the Lynchs' extended period when 'not any one is [. . .] any where near to any dying' (718) comes to an abrupt end with the death of 'Liz wife of Sam' (Beckett, 2009f, 88).

Both texts also make interesting use of cardinal numbers, with these same numbers proving of little use in progressing or advancing our knowledge of the events described. The impediments to Watt and Mrs Gorman's physical interactions, for example, are conveyed by listing the number of physical readjustments Watt was at times required to make: 'And so little could Watt support, on certain days, [. . .] that no fewer than two, or three, or four, or five, or six, or seven, or eight, or nine, or ten, or eleven, or even twelve, or even thirteen, changes of position were found necessary' (Beckett, 2009f, 121).

Just as Beckett's use of the conjunctional 'or' serves to prevent any specific number or position marking itself out as distinct from another, in the phrase 'one and then another and then another one and then another one said something and then some other one said something and some one can listen to every one who says something' (1995, 730) Stein exploits the semantic crossover between the cardinal number 'one' and its pronominal namesake, employing the determiners 'another' and 'some' to create complex instances of specific non-specificity. These permutations are identical to many found throughout *Watt*, as, for example, in the following description of the different days of the week any individual may have a preference for, which concludes with the rather Stein-like anti-summation that some people like some days, and other people like other days: 'So Thursday was the day Watt preferred, to all other days. Some prefer Sunday, others Monday, others Tuesday, others Wednesday, others Friday, others Saturday' (Beckett, 2009f, 120). Each new iteration is merely an addition to the cumulative renarrative cycles Beckett and Stein have built via the careful manipulation of recurring conjunctions and determiners: 'or' in Beckett's case, 'one' in Stein's. Taken together, they create sequences wherein both totality and specificity are impossible, impeded as they are by this consistent deferring of meaning brought about by an apparent inability to settle on or secure even the most banal and non-committal of meanings.

Elsewhere, Stein uses a combination of the determiner 'another' with the pronoun 'one' when listing groups of people who are in varying states of agreement with her narrator:

> I am not believing this thing, another one is not believing this thing, another one is not believing this thing, another one is believing this thing, another one is believing this thing, another one is believing this thing, another one is believing this thing, another one is not believing this thing, another one is not believing this thing. (Stein, 1995, 728)

The pronominally tenuous listener/hearer dyad presented throughout Stein's account here of a 'one [who] can listen to every one who says something' (730) can be compared to similar situations in many of Beckett's later fictions, particularly the *Nohow On* texts, as the following example from *Company* makes explicit: 'If the voice is not speaking to him it must be speaking to another. So with what reason remains he reasons. To another of that other. Or of him. Or of another still. To another of that other or of him or of another still' (Beckett, 2009a, 6). Similarly, Stein's declaration of intent regarding the procession of her narrative, wherein she states, 'and I will give one description and then another description and then another description and then another description of the being in him' (Stein, 1995, 734), bears comparison with *Molloy*: 'This time, then once more I think, then perhaps a last time, then I think it'll be over, with the world too. Premonition of the last but one but one' (Beckett, 2009d, 4).

The following passage from *The Making of Americans* sees something of a culmination of this technique, with the semantic meaning of 'one' moving from the numerical to the pronominal and vice versa in almost every sentence:

> He was often then with one. He was often then with three. He was often then with two. He was often then with three. He was often then with another one. He was often then with six. He was often then with ten. He was often then with one. He was often then with another one. He was often then with another one. He was often then with another one. He was often then with three. (1995, 854–5).

Flexible modifiers such as 'another', 'more' and 'any', capable of operating as determiners, pronouns or adverbs, are used to create ambiguous portraits of the number of other 'ones' this 'he' (who is in fact the novel's protagonist, David Hersland) was 'often then with'. Stein's oblique accounts of the various 'ones' that populate her narrative here merit immediate comparison with the speculative future occupants of the Knott household in *Watt*:

> [A]nd a man come, shutting the door behind him, and Erskine go. And then another night fall and another man come and Watt go, Watt who is now come, for the coming is in the shadow of the going and the going is in the shadow of the coming, that is the annoying part about it. (Beckett, 2009f, 48)

Two pages later this is taken further with a lengthier account that reaches instead into the unknown past, reflecting on the unknown (by name) occupants who inhabited the house before Vincent and Walter:

> For Vincent and Walter were not the first, ho no, but before them were Vincent and another whose name I forget, and before them that other whose name I forget and another whose name I also forget [. . .] and so on, until all trace is lost. (Beckett, 2009f, 50)

This again has a counterpart in Stein's text, at the point where the narrator resolves to extend the remit of her study of every human being that exists or has ever existed, including those yet to be, those not yet in existence, or those who hold a speculative or conditional chance of coming into existence; figures that can be classified as speculative or future conditional 'ones', as Stein similarly pursues these traces until they are lost: 'I am almost being certain that I am understanding all being ever having been, ever being, ever going to be in any man, in any woman' (1995, 684).

For all its detail, much of the information contained throughout *Watt* and *The Making of Americans* is itself useless, managing the dual task of being extraordinarily specific and nondescript at the same time. Any implication of specificity as a result of this intense scrutiny brought about by the repetitions is prevented through the abundance of meanings heaped on the word by the renarrative act. As the narrator of Stein's text observes, 'It is very interesting, often very exciting, mostly very confusing, always steadily increasing in meaning' (1995, 335). While the first two terms in this description are debatable, the final two are certainties, for throughout both *Watt* and *The Making of Americans* the narratives proceed in a manner that is 'mostly very confusing' and 'always steadily increasing in meaning' (335).

Beyond these similarities in terms of their respective narrative strategies, the root inquisitiveness that propels the narrator of *The Making of Americans* – who admits, some 556 pages into her novel, to belonging to the category of 'men and women [who] are inquisitive about everything' (Stein, 1995, 556) – is very comparable to similar instances of inquisitiveness and speculation found throughout *Watt*. Just as Watt's inquisitiveness regarding Mr Knott's daily routine and eating habits (Beckett, 2009f, 71–5) or indeed, his decision that 'an examination of Erskine's room was essential, if his mind was to be pacified, in this connexion' (105), is responsible for his subsequent discovery of and interest in the painting in Erskine's room (109–10), Stein's narrator belongs to the category of people who 'if they see any one with anything they ask, what is that thing, what is it you are carrying, what are you going to be doing with that thing, why do you have that thing, where did you get that thing, how long will you have that thing' (Stein, 1995, 556). These can all be placed in counterpoint with the declaration that this pursuit of meaning was enacted in spite of a general indifference to meaning (Beckett, 2009f, 62), an unusual scenario that again has a counterexample in Stein and the narrator's pronouncement that 'it all grows confusing [. . .] sometimes all of a sudden I lose the meaning out of all of them I lose all of them [. . .] and there is no meaning' (Stein, 1995, 335).

Like that of *The Making of Americans*, the text of *Watt* contains numerous unresolved issues or unknowable events and abundant examples of words that come under increasing scrutiny and seem to bear little real relationship to what it is they supposedly signify. 'How can anything be different from what it is?', Stein's narrator asks (1995, 672). Beckett conducts similarly relentless interrogations of the relationship between 'Watt's hat', '[y]our hat', 'the hat' and 'his hat' (2009f, 20), between 'a dog' and 'the dog' (80). So we have a situation wherein, as Stein puts it 'everything being what it is, everything not being what it is, something being what it is, nothing being what it is' (1995, 672). Similarly, uncertainty rounds off the text of *Watt* with the closing line 'no symbols where none intended' (Beckett, 2009f, 223); a closing statement that serves to create a retroactive haze of uncertainty throughout an already difficult text. One thing we can be certain of, then, in relation to both *The Making of Americans* and *Watt*, is the ever-present presence of uncertainty.

In *Watt* and *The Making of Americans* Beckett and Stein take to task specific aspects of the English language they found problematic and hindering to their attempts at writing in English. In *The Making of Americans* Stein uses machinations of the English language to render the language of her prose insufficient as a communicative entity, sabotaging the facultative elements of the English language and inhibiting words and word phrases from relaying that which they are ostensibly supposed to relay. She does so by harnessing the technique of repetition and adapting it to serve as an acute and precise tool for destabilising the English language in the form of specific and deliberate renarrations. The shells of word forms themselves are exploited throughout these novels, with Stein opting to extrapolate the full spectrum of signification potentials from her chosen word forms; testing the boundaries of meaning, testing the medium itself. 'The complete gamut of variation' (Stein, 1995, 474) of a given term is identical in appearance to that same term merely being repeated over and over and over again.

In contrast to Stein's provocation of the infinite or 'complete gamut of variation' in her tirade against facultative language use, Beckett approaches this task in a more restrained manner throughout *Watt*, working within a more finite, bilingual system. The result, as Slote puts it, is 'an English inflected by French', and one wherein 'French echoes, such as the 'facultative stop' [...] (after art facultatif)' is employed as a means of 'conveying this uncertainty' (2015, 118). That Watt's entry into the text of *Watt* occurs via his unceremonious ejection from a tram at this 'merely facultative stop' (Beckett, 2009f, 13) can be taken as a statement of intent: Beginning at an end point, starting at a forced stop, and one that speaks across two languages, Beckett's renarrative praxis throughout *Watt* is notable, and notably distinct from Stein's, precisely because the destabilising effect of renarration on a term's facultative meaning is situated within a nascent English-French bilingual network. The result, as Slote notes, is a language that is '*not quite* English' (Slote, 2015, 118), with this 'not quite' often traceable to French terms or expressions. Stein, in contrast, does not supply this cipher, relentlessly 'exploding all syntactic rules' and refusing what Perloff refers to as the 'illusion' of 'syntactic order' in Beckett's sentences (Perloff, 1999, 209). By subjecting the language to rigorous renarrations, both authors transgress the limitations of English grammar by exposing them to excessive semantic and syntactic stresses designed to instigate the metaphoric tears or porosities Beckett mentions throughout the 1937 Kaun letter.

Stein's *not quite* English is thus more extreme than Beckett's, even if their renarrative praxes are proximate. Rather than inflecting her work with words that harbour French connotations, as Beckett does, Stein instead relies on non-committal but multivalent words, taking advantage of and harnessing the gamut of semantic potential latent in these simple language units, the minima that not only distinguished her work from that of Joyce, but made that same work attractive to Beckett. Every statement 'towards the specific becomes a statement of infinite variations within a system of infinite variants. We are continually reminded that, even without authorial trickery or clever repetitions, the exact meaning of a word changes from person to person. It is important here to observe too that logographs and logography – the Steinian technique Beckett cites in the Kaun letter – are themselves a very basic form of synonymic renarration (wherein the repeated term is replaced with a synonym of itself), one of the predominant facets at work throughout the technical machinations of *Watt* and *The Making of Americans*. This, again, is Beckett's 'no symbols where none intended' (2009f, 223) put to work in the very body of a prose text.

4 Getting Mixed: Lexical Renarrations

> I like to write with prepositions and conjunctions and articles and verbs and adverbs but not with nouns and adjectives. (Stein, 1998, 316)

Nominalistic irony is central to Beckett's praise (and critique) of Stein in 1937, with attacks on English grammar of the kind identifiable in her logographs a 'necessary phase' in the discrediting of language (Beckett, 2009c, 520). While the extrovert and esoteric logographs throughout *Tender Buttons* are her best-known example of logographic subversion, Stein's attack on normative language use extended beyond the noun to every facet of the sentence. This section will examine the comparable nature of Beckett and Stein's engagement in lexical renarrations at the level of the sentence, covering nouns, verbs and pronouns.

4.1 Nouns and Adjectives: 'Forthwith the Uncommon Common Noun Collapsion'[9]

Stein's distaste for the noun is made abundantly clear in her lecture 'Poetry and Grammar', where she queries the need for them in writing at all, asking 'Why write in nouns' (1998, 313). She declares them 'by definition completely not interesting' (314) and later, in *How to Write*, claims 'There should not be

---

[9] Beckett, 2009a, 83.

a noun' (1975, 146). Perloff picks up on this nominal ambivalence and presents it in the context of Stein's contemporaries, noting that while 'the noun or noun phrase was obviously central to Eliot [. . .] and even more so to Pound [. . .] Stein regularly dismissed the noun as the least interesting part of speech' (2002, 64–5). Despite this ambivalence, however, for an extended period during the 1910s, a period during which Stein produced works such as *Tender Buttons*, Stein looked extensively at nominal word forms and specifically experimented with the idea of providing replacement titles for nouns already in existence – nouns Stein deemed insufficient and unsatisfactory.[10]

In 1937 Beckett refers to '[w]ord-storming' (2009c, 520) as a necessary step towards his desired aesthetics. Accordingly, common nouns are exposed to almost relentless renarrative scrutiny throughout *Watt*, with Beckett (like Stein before him) employing renarrative strategies at the level of the sentence in order to induce what the narrator of *Ill Seen Ill Said* would later refer to as a 'noun collapsion' (2009a, 83). The first example comes in the form of Watt's smile: '[I]t was true that Watt's smile, when he smiled, resembled more a smile than a sneer, for example, or a yawn. [. . .] To many it seemed a simple sucking of teeth' (2009f, 19). Watt's smile is presented in terms of what it is not, with this anti-description further obscured by the statement that it would perhaps be more accurate to consider it a 'sucking of teeth' (19). A more elaborate process occurs in 'Text for Nothing II' in the form of antonymic renarration with respect to adjectives used to describe moisture levels: 'Dry, it's possible, or wet, or slime, as before matter took ill' (2009e, 8). The level of moisture varies dramatically following every iteration of the conjunction 'or', from dry to the antonymic wet followed by an apparent middle ground or synthesis in the form of 'slime'. While the sentence could itself be labelled a denarration, doing so diminished the importance of the synergic term 'slime' as a sort of midpoint between dryness and wetness; one that could only have been enabled by a renarrative strategy as opposed to a twofold denarration.

The following example, this time from *How to Write*, sees Stein employ antonymic adjectives in tandem through a form of semantic epanalepsis where both antonyms are declared equally pertinent to the description: 'The door was open as well as closed' (1975, 106). This sentence enacts a situation wherein the semantic content of two oppositional adjectives modifying a head term (in this instance, 'door') are declared equivocal. While its most obvious comparison is perhaps the door sequence at the beginning of *Watt*, where Watt attempts to

---

[10] Not only is it likely that *Tender Buttons* is the text Beckett has in mind when speaking of Stein's logographs in his letter to Kaun of 1937, *Tender Buttons* is also the work Stein refers to in 'A Transatlantic Interview–1946' as the apex of the period in her writing life when she felt particularly ambivalent towards nouns. It is this very ambivalence and distrust that Beckett singles out for particular attention in the letter.

discern why 'the back door, so lately locked, [was] now open' (Beckett, 2009f, 29), this sequence relies less on modifiers and more on a series of logical elaborations, and so can be considered a less efficient example of the type of strategic tearing Beckett was working towards, if it is that at all. Instead, a more fitting comparison is found in *How It Is*, where the antonyms beginning and end are, like Stein's open and closed door, declared analogous: 'two possible formulations therefore the present and that other beginning where the present ends' (Beckett, 2009b, 115).

Just as both authors employ renarration to manipulate named nouns, so too can they manipulate unnamed or non-specific nouns. Each transition of the named but non-specific sacks from figure to figure throughout Beckett's *How It Is*, for example, is mirrored and enabled by a similar transition of 'things' that 'nameless [. . .] awaits' and 'nameless goes towards' their next interlocutor: 'the same voice the same things nothing changing but the names and hardly they two are enough nameless each awaits his Bom nameless goes towards his Pim' (2009b, 99). What changes is not so much the 'names and hardly they' but rather the attributes that surround and further modify the unnamed figures. For comparison, consider the following passage from Stein's *How to Write*:

> He said does it please you that they have a name. He says yes it does as everybody has a name. He is spoken of by his name. Does it please you that he is spoken of by a name and that that name is his name. He is spoken of by his name. (Stein, 1975, 206)

As in the nameless transition of figures throughout Beckett's *How It Is*, the name in this passage (in this instance, literally, the name 'name') remains consistent, but the term immediately preceding every iteration of the name changes, with the name 'that is his name' never revealed. All we can be sure of, at most, is the pleonastic assertion 'that he is spoken of by a name and that that name is his name', an intimation of specificity that instead reinforces Stein's tenet that a noun may name one particular thing, but it can also name anything: 'A noun is the name of anything' (1975, 20). There is a remarkable proximity between this sentiment and that of the narrator in 'Text for Nothing VI' who asks 'what is it, this unnamable thing that I name and name and never wear out, and I call that words. [. . .] with what words shall I name my unnamable words?' (Beckett, 2009e, 27–8). Beckett stresses the ontological facet of these problems of naming through his penchant for repeatedly emphasising that this parade of various 'things' is symptomatic of the unnamability of these same terms. Stein, in contrast, never quite goes so far as to make her procession of problematic 'things' explicitly ontological.

At the same time, however, Beckett's presentation of an 'unnamable thing' (2009e, 29) that is named yet unnamable sees its counterpart in Stein's portrait of a similar such 'thing' from *Tender Buttons*: 'a red thing not a round thing but a white thing, a red thing and a white thing' (Stein, 2014, 12). This time, however, in contrast with the clear demarcations Beckett laid out to distinguish his different 'things' in our previous examples, or indeed the distinctions Stein imported onto different 'somethings' throughout *The Making of Americans*, it is unclear whether the 'red thing' and 'white thing' refer to distinct or indistinct things. Again, this can be considered a point of contrast: Beckett's prose maintains a semantic integrity, a belief that it is, perhaps, merely a case that the narrators 'haven't hit on the right ones, the killers' (Beckett, 2009e, 27–8), whereas Stein's prose, in contrast, is actively degrading the rules of grammar and style as she employs them. Thus, an object in *Tender Buttons* supposedly displays 'a white way of being round' (Stein, 2014, 13), but within the epistemology of standard English language, this effectively makes no sense – what does it mean for something to be round in a white way? Yet in embodying this nonsense on a semantic level, she effectively not only demonstrates her distrust of the major grammatical modifiers, but illustrates the very limits of their use. As both authors have made abundantly clear, a noun can be the name of anything, and each apparent specification regarding 'anything' is of limited value as, in asking about 'anything' one could be asking about 'everything' and vice versa.

Nouns and adjectives thus play an integral role as a grammatical modifier in the work of both authors, serving to blur the lines that distinguish foreground from background, object from surround, and even to make certain objects dissimilar from themselves. Much of what is presented in this respect in the examples shown here is, like aspects of the foods and objects of *Tender Buttons*, narrated and subsequently renarrated as 'the same sight slighter' (Stein, 2014, 13). The changes that take place as a result of these renarrational modifications serve to retroactively tear at the semantic certainties in the descriptive terms used. Beckett and Stein prioritise terms that delimit or specify, only to then demonstrate the inherently unquantifiable nature of any and all attempts to make these terms quantitative; so much so that, like Watt, one can at best hope to ascertain 'What was changed, if my information is correct, was the sentiment that a change, other than a change of degree, had taken place' (Beckett, 2009f, 36).

4.2 Verbs: 'Every One I Have Been Describing I Will Be Describing I Am Describing'[11]

Verbs may be responsible for 'the inevitable narrative of anything', together with the 'feeling that anything that everything had meaning as beginning and middle and ending' (Stein, 2010, 25), but Stein nevertheless indicates a strong preference

---

[11] Stein, 1995, 551.

for them in her writings. In 'Poetry and Grammar' she speaks of having 'recognise[d] verbs and adverbs aided by prepositions and conjunctions with pronouns as possessing the whole of the active life of writing' (1998, 320). This preference is born from what Stein classifies as their imprecision, citing them as useful to her in her writings because they frequently err. 'It is wonderful the number of mistakes a verb can make', Stein states. 'Verbs can be so [mistaken] endlessly, both as to what they do and how they agree or disagree with whatever they do. The same is true of adverbs' (314). To engage in traditional modes of narration is to make use of, be bound by, the inherent temporal falsities that accompany verb tense, falsities enhanced by adverbial suggestion.

While Beckett does not go so far as to explicitly praise the error-prone nature of verbs, as Stein does, his narrators make frequent commentaries regarding their dissatisfaction with verb tense, such as Molloy's directive that 'This should all be rewritten in the pluperfect' (Beckett, 2009d, 13) or the plea for 'a little less of to be present past future and conditional of to be and not to be' (2009b, 31) from *How It Is*, noted earlier. Similarly, as Beckett's narrator suggests elsewhere in *Texts for Nothing*, engaging in modes of narration that contain implicit temporal markers is to become 'dupes of every time and tense': 'Yes, no more denials, all is false, there is no one, it's understood, no more phrases, let us be dupes, dupes of every time and tense' (2009d, 11). Both authors actively work against such duping, such 'inevitable narratives' (Stein, 2010, 25), by engaging in explicit renarrative praxes that subvert normative grammatical verb and tense use in narrative. For example, in the following excerpt from 'Text for Nothing IV', Beckett seems to be attempting to move beyond the 'inevitable' beginnings, middles and endings of narrative so criticised by Stein:

> Then it all goes, all goes, and I'm far again, with a far story again, I wait for me afar for my story to begin, to end, and again this voice cannot be mine. That's where I'd go, if I could go, that's who I'd be, if I could be. (Beckett, 2009d, 19)

This creation of a narrative space wherein time is uncertain – as are the differentiations between the concordant terms beginning and ending, being and non-being – is accomplished not through abstractions but through a controlled use of conjunctions in tandem with the strategic use of modal verbs. The resulting effect of mingled tenses may induce confusion, but the mingling itself is not random or chaotic. Rather it proceeds by meticulous approaches to restating the already said, hallmarks of both authors' renarrative styles.

While Montini observes that 'L'histoire telle que Watt la raconta n'a de logique temporelle ni spatiale [The story Watt recounts has neither temporal nor spatial logic] (2007, 144; my translation), such illogical temporal and spatial narratives continue through to Beckett's later writings, the texts

Montini classifies as 'bilingually francophone' (178).[12] 'Text for Nothing I' makes explicit reference to states of temporal melding similar to those found throughout *How It Is* wherein: 'All mingles, times and tenses, at first I only had been here, now I'm here still, soon I won't be here yet, [. . .] for the moment I'm here, always have been, always shall be' (Beckett, 2009d, 5).

The mingling of times and tenses occurs simultaneously throughout this passage, together with an additional querying of place, discussed shortly. This occurs by virtue of the fact that the verbs used are explicitly related to the act of relaying time, with definite changes of temporality suggested by a change of verb tense. The 'head' or source terms from which the resulting modifications develop comes in the form of the statement 'at first I only had been here'. The adverb 'still' indicates a temporal shift, with a transition from just arrived ('I only had been here') to being 'still' there, as implied by the phrase 'now I'm here still'. Finally, the adverb 'soon' and associated statement 'soon I won't be here' seem to indicate a progression to a further state, the state of not being 'here'. But this assertion is thrown awry by the adverb 'yet', thus suggesting the figure is not yet there, despite the fact that they have just asserted they are 'still here'. Carrying on, the progression appears to reset and revert to asserting a definite presence 'here' 'for the moment', followed by a double recurrence of the adverb 'always', employed to imply a state of perpetual presence: 'I'm here, always have been, always shall be.' In this way, Beckett manages to instil uncertainty into the narrative representations of both time and place by means of relatively straightforward verbal and adverbial renarrative modifications.

Aside from instances of single-word repetition of verbs wherein the verb is repeated unchanged or with a slight modification to tense, both authors employ renarrative elaborations that make use of antonyms of the head term. In the following two examples relating to movement, one from each author, this serves to infuse the act of movement with a curious stasis, presenting the act of progress by means of forward motion as counteractive and asymptotic:

> Any time they go they stay. (Stein, 1975, 20)

> She still without stopping. On her way without starting. Gone without going.
> Back without returning. (Beckett, 2009a, 53)

These two passages are all but identical in sentiment and technical execution. Both stand out as instances of finely distilled, strategic renarration that disrupt the semantic fabric of their respective statements, so that each verbal progression is

---

[12] All translations from Montini in this Element are my own.

followed by a regression in an improbable narrative space that is perpetually 'Toward but never nearer' (Beckett, 2009a 55).

Beyond temporality, depictions of place by means of verbs relating to movement or journeying towards or away from a specific place give rise to some of the most frequently observed instances of renarration involving verbal and adverbial modifiers in Beckett and Stein. Renarration can, as Stein puts it in *How To Write*, engender scenarios wherein here and there appear synchronous, as in the statement 'From here from here in from there to there' (Stein, 1975, 53). Stein melds differential adverbially constructed places in her exposure of the adverbs 'here' and 'there' to an aporetic scenario wherein 'here' and 'there' are shown to be semantically (and thus geographically) homogenous:

> From here from here in from there to there.
> From here.
> From here from here to from here to there. (1975, 53)

This relatively straightforward manipulation of the anagrammatic and phonemic relationship between 'here' and 'there' problematises the spatial distinction supposedly relayed by the adverbs 'here' and 'there' by presenting them as equivalent, inviting a reading that sees 'here' in 'there'. Stein's equating of 'here' and 'there' can here be contrasted with her famous observation 'not there, there is no there there' (Stein, 1973, 289) from *Everybody's Autobiography* (1937), or indeed Beckett's 'Somewhere on the Ballyogan Road in lieu of nowhere in particular' (Beckett, 2009a, 14).

While Stein may find 'here' in 'there' but struggle to locate a 'there' in 'there', Beckett's narrator in the following much-quoted passage from 'Text for Nothing III' manages to be here, far from here, and there: 'I'll be there, I won't miss it, it won't be me, I'll be here, I'll say I'm far from here, it won't be me' (Beckett, 2009e, 11). Uncertainty regarding the ability to be truly 'here' is also a feature of 'Text for Nothing VI' and 'Text for Nothing IX' respectively: 'I'd join them with a will if it could be here and now, how is it nothing is ever here and now?'; 'now, now that I'm here, if I'm here, and no longer there, coming and going' (25, 39). In the first example, the coexistence of temporal immediacy and spatial presence found in the 'here and now' is declared impossible through the use of the modal 'could' together with the conjunction 'if'. In the second, the narrator first tentatively situates himself as being 'here' before the conjunctive 'if' queries this 'here', while the reintroduction of the adverb 'there' again makes these two places distinct.

The apparent inconclusiveness of the here/there adverbs comes to read as deliberate incitements to err, an action that, as Stein notes, is a particular habitude of verbal and adverbial modifiers. This is something Beckett similarly seems to note and capitalise on in relation to his treatment of the verbs and adverbs relating to place, as can be seen from his suggestion that, much like the 'no symbols where none intended' of *Watt* (2009f, 223), distinctions of place all amount to something of an 'infinite here': 'Elsewhere perhaps, by all means, elsewhere, what elsewhere can there be to this infinite here?' (2009e, 25). Similarly, Stein declares in 'An Elucidation' that there is 'in a place a place for everything': 'Place, in a place. A place for everything and everything in its place. In place a place for everything, in a place' (Stein, 1996, 431).

Many of these statements can be classified as tautological. Here again there is room for explicit comparison between Stein and Beckett as can be seen when the following two observations from *How to Write* are placed alongside a single, similarly tautological example from *How It Is*:

> Wait for what you are waiting for. (Stein, 1975, 31)

> Forget with or without. With or without forget with or without. Forget to forget to forget with or without. (152)

> nothing ever as much as begun, nothing ever but nothing and never, nothing ever but lifeless words. (Beckett, 2009e, 50)

Aside from labelling such passages as deliberate tautologies, in the context of Beckett and Stein's shared dissatisfactions with received language, it is further evidence of the extreme and exacting attention they paid to the grammars of the languages they wrote in, asking questions of the most banal terms, such as, as in this example, whether the act of waiting entails waiting, or whether a verb such as 'to wait' or 'waiting' is inherently related to the act of 'waiting'. The lines 'when he sets out to seek out all of him sets out to seek out the true home' (Beckett, 2009b, 89) from Beckett and 'Premeditated. That is meditated before meditation' (Stein, 1975, 32), from Stein are further examples of this shared concern. Each clearly shows the authors' deliberate manipulation of the semantics and functional tasks of the verbs and adverbs they employ so as to undermine their semantic and functional efficacy, using language against language in a full-scale assault on the 'Grammar and style!' of 'formal English' that has clearly moved beyond the demonstrations of 'nominalistic irony' (2009c, 520) Beckett begrudgingly embraces in 1937.

4.3 Pronouns: 'Homeless mes and untenanted hims'[13]

The previous two sections made clear the comparable nature of Beckett and Stein's manipulations of major grammatical modifiers of the kind Banfield classified as the 'productive categories' (2003, 16) – the nouns and adjectives,

---

[13] Beckett, 2009e, 50.

verbs and adverbs Joseph Emonds in turn refers to as the 'mental lexicon which consists of the open classes of the more contentful lexical items' (2001, vii) – and the strategies adopted by both authors so as to bring about a subversion of these 'contentful' open-class lexical terms. The concluding section now takes as its topic what Banfield, drawing on the work of Emond, refers to as 'nonproductive' modifiers, and what Emond himself classifies as the 'grammatical lexicon bereft of purely semantic features' (vii). Banfield sees Beckett's engagement with these lesser modifiers as particular to his late style, while also identifying his engagement with the same as a point of contrast with Joyce. 'Noun, Verb, Adjective/Adverb, language's so-called content words', Banfield writes, were the 'aspect of language exploited by Joyce's "revolution of the word"' (2003, 15). In the context of an aesthetics of language that has its foundations in an expressed distaste for 'Grammar and style!', together with a concordant desire, as Beckett puts it, to both abuse language and 'contribute to its disrepute' (Beckett, 2009c, 518), a more productive avenue is found by capitalising on '"closed-class" lexical formatives – grammatical "function words" like determiners, pronouns, and so on' (Banfield, 2003, 16). An attack on the sense-making capacity of language would therefore be better served (or more 'efficiently abused'; Beckett, 2009c, 518) through an approach that capitalises on these already semantically tenuous and changeable terms, terms that are themselves already 'made porous' (518) referring as they do to particularly 'nonproductive' semantic terms.

Pronouns and the manipulation of pronouns present both authors with opportunities for continuing their respective tearing at the fabric of language on a more acute – and arguably more effective – scale. While Stein relegated the noun to the position of the lexically least interesting, her assessment of the pronoun was not so severe. 'Pronouns are not as bad as nouns', she argues in 'Poetry and Grammar', because 'they are not really the name of anything. They represent someone but they are not its or his name' (1998, 316). Like Beckett after her, Stein capitalised on this pronominal ambiguity, perhaps seeing in it an opportunity similar to the capacity to err that so appealed to her when it came to the use of verbs and adverbs in narrative. Again, a direct equation is made between their usefulness to her and what she perceives as their capacity to obfuscate or 'not really' 'name anything' (316). Their reach and flexibility extends far beyond that of the standard common noun and can alternately refer to something or nothing, to a specific one, anyone, everyone, someone or no one, a fact that grants them greater potential as tools in the strategic tearing of language through renarrative modifications.

The opening paragraph of *The Making of Americans* sees Stein establish an improbable scenario relating to inherited behaviours and a familial trait for paternal battery: 'Once an angry man dragged his father along the ground through his own orchard. "Stop!" cried the groaning old man at last, "Stop! I did not drag my father beyond this tree"' (1995, 3). This is comparable to a line from Beckett's 'Text for Nothing I', where distinct pronouns are paired to achieve repetition in the form of an intergenerational memory of rheumatism: 'My rheumatism in any case is no more than a memory, it hurts me no more than my mother's did, when it hurt her' (Beckett, 2009e, 5). Whereas hereditary rheumatism in and of itself is hardly novel, this is not the generational tie that is stressed here; rather, the narrator emphasises a sort-of intergenerational memory. This process reoccurs in the concluding passage of the same text, this time in relation to the narrator's father and son: 'Yes, I was my father and I was my son, I asked myself questions and answered as best I could, I had it told me evening after evening, the same old story I knew by heart' (6). Here again we see the same process, with the first-person pronoun 'I' and the possessive determiner 'my' repeated and paired with semantically incompatible nouns to create a sentence that is grammatically correct but semantically and biologically impossible (except perhaps within the 'fortunate [and incestuous] family Lynch' (Beckett, 2009f, 84)). A more efficient example occurs later in 'Text for Nothing XII' with the observation 'it's me in him remembering' (2009e, 49). To refer back to an example discussed at the end of the previous section, these examples are identical in their technical execution to the seemingly incompatible semantic pairings that make a clause like 'a white way of being round' (Stein, 2014, 13) impossible to reconcile semantically.

Similar too are the following examples, the first from 'Text for Nothing VII', the second from 'Saving the Sentence' in Stein's *How to Write*:

> I'd like to be sure I left no stone unturned before reporting me missing and giving up. (Beckett, 2009e, 29)

> I do not know nor do I know if he thinks with them or without me. (Stein, 1975, 19)

These examples are interesting for their apparent doubling or splitting of the speaker's identity. In the first instance, from Beckett, the speaker shows a capacity to comment on activities of the self while also commenting on a certain absence of self ('me' is missing but the event is reported by 'I'). The second example, from Stein, displays a seemingly dual 'I-figure' brought about by the repetition of the pronoun 'I' with both made distinct by means of the adverb 'nor'. Similar again, the two occurrences of 'they' in 'They are different they and I' (Stein, 1975, 190), together with the 'I'll be here, I'll say I'm far from here' (Beckett, 2009e, 11) invite us to remember Stein's earlier iteration that 'There is no reason why they should compare them with themselves' (1975, 125).

Both authors show preference for different pronouns, with Beckett specifically engaged in the manipulation of personal pronouns (as well as the more ambiguous 'other' that haunts his later fictions), and Stein, in contrast, displaying a tendency to employ generalist pronouns such as 'some', 'one' and 'another', terms that straddle the general and the specific and enable her exploration of the 'complete gamut of variation' (Stein, 1995, 474) throughout *The Making of Americans*. Despite this, the methods adopted for engendering a diffusion of the distinctions between different 'ones' or different 'others' and conversely, the methods employed to indicate similitude or sameness between others, are identical. Consider the following concentrated instances of pronominal confusion (what Cordingley refers to as a 'confusion of pronouns'; 2007, 188) found throughout *How It Is*:

> who for me for whom I what I for Pim Pim for me [;]

> to whom of whom to whom of me of whom to me

> Bom to the abandoned not me Bom you Bom we Bom but me Bom you Pim
> I to the abandoned not me Pim you Pim we Pim but me Bom you Pim.
> (Beckett, 2009b, 52; 93; 100)

When placed alongside an excerpt from Stein's essay 'Sentences', their writings appear fascinatingly proximate to the point where it becomes difficult to tell who authored which:

> For theirs. That is an idea. This is for them. That is hers. That is hers for this
> for theirs that which they have for them. They have this for them. This is hers
> for theirs theirs for hers with this for hers this for theirs with for hers. With
> her. (Stein, 1975, 128)

In Section 2's discussion of their non-fiction writings on language, Stein's enumerative lists of grammatical articles were presented as examples of her fascination with the materiality of language. Here, when placed alongside Beckett's fusillades between Bom and Pim, they read as pronominally overabundant sentences wherein the narrative impetus is firmly situated in the realm of pronominal and determiner-focussed clauses. Similarly, Beckett's pronoun sentences read like enumerative lists that would not themselves be out of place in a Steinian grammar workbook. That Stein is aligning the narrative impetus with pronouns and determiners (as opposed to verbs and nouns) is confirmed by the puzzling aphorism that immediately follows the passage just quoted, an aphorism that would not be out of place as an epigram for *Texts for Nothing*: 'In this the pronouns do not count they are only the story. The pronouns in this do not count they are only the story' (Stein, 1975, 128). Stein appears to be suggesting a narrative state akin to that encountered throughout *The Unnamable* wherein 'affirmations and negations [are] invalidated as uttered, or sooner or later' (Beckett, 2010, 3).

That Beckett and Stein were following markedly similar aesthetic strategies regarding the creation of semantically insecure statements, that they were actualising these strategies in the form of specific techniques involving the modification of the grammars and syntaxes of sentences, should now be explicit. Similarly clear is the comparable nature of Stein's attempts at subverting 'the inevitable narrative of anything' (2010, 24–5) and Beckett's seeming actualisation of this throughout *Texts for Nothing* and elsewhere, through their respective subversions of temporal and semantic certainty via verbal, nominal and pronominal renarrations. Beckett's narratives, particularly in *Texts for Nothing* (i.e. post *The Unnamable*), seem to exist at or beyond just such a point, namely the point where one can distinguish between beginning, middle and ending. Similar too are their pragmatic approaches to the application of verbs, adverbs, nouns and adjectives in repetitive patterns that facilitate semantic indeterminacy.

These renarrative elaborations frequently take on the characteristics of the rhetorical epanorthosis, with each iteration discrediting the preceding sentence or statement by renarrating it so that it reappears in a slightly modified format. The trigger for each redaction in these examples appears to be a dissatisfaction with a term used in the first iteration. Each restatement involves a modification to that preceding term, be that in the form of tense change (temporal), a change from positive to negative, or a semantic recalibration to reflect an alternative (often semantically oppositional or antonymic) position. Stability of semantic meaning in one aspect of the statement enables the introduction of semantic indeterminacy in the other; in order to enable semantic modification at least one aspect of the sentence or passage needs to retain stability, functioning as an anchoring device so the reader can identify the grammatical indiscretion when and where it occurs and register its effect on the surrounding narrative. In the writings of both authors this is performed with almost surgical precision, and while this is something of a characteristic of Beckett's work, it has not always been considered characteristic of Stein's. The previous sections have made explicit, however, that while Stein is certainly less concerned with maintaining semantic sense throughout a given sentence or passage, her endeavours to undermine semantic certainties are enacted in a meticulous manner by means of systematic redactions and modifications to an initial phrasal assertion. When delineated, these systematised renarrations are as procedural as Beckett's own.

Renarration at the level of the sentence presents perhaps the most efficient (remembering Beckett's emphasis on efficiency in his 1937 letter to Kaun) avenue through which to enact a tearing at the seams of language and semantic sense. It also, in the case of Stein in particular, takes the linguistic sabotaging away from the world of inanimate objects of the kind found throughout *Tender Buttons*. These nominal revisions arguably have limited subversive potential because, irrespective of their efficacy in remaking the noun, their range is restricted by the nominal terms in and of themselves. Rather, as this section has made clear, aesthetic and technical proximity in relation to the literary techniques and styles of both authors extends beyond the noun and is found in their respective renarrations of other grammatical modifiers at the level of the sentence. In adopting the same techniques, their work produces remarkably similar results, or, as Stein puts it in 'Composition as Explanation', 'everything being alike and everything being simply different' (2004, 28).

5 Lexical Renarrations and the Goodbye to Standard English: Stein's Role in the Development of Beckett's Bilingual English Praxis

> Now in English they mean very well for once.
> Now translate that to now in English they mean very well for once (Stein, 1975, 17)

Read purely from the point of view of Beckett's aesthetic development, and with a view to eschewing the tendency to fall into the coterie-driven divisions that have impeded a full appreciation of Beckett and Stein's comparable styles, Beckett's letter to Kaun in 1937 clearly demonstrates his move away from a particular mode of writing that disrupted the English language by importing non-English terms – what Montini classifies as 'monolingual polyglottism' (2007, 33) – and towards a mode of writing that affected similar semantic disturbances through syntactic manipulations in ostensibly unilingual situations. Stein's work was a key touchstone or pivot point in Beckett's transition away from a Joycean 'monolingual polyglottism' (Montini, 2007, 33) and towards what Montini classifies as 'le bilinguisme anglophone [bilingual anglophone]' (95), which in itself was an integral step in Beckett's transition towards the French-authored texts that made his name and the development of a fully bilingual oeuvre that saw him working in – and between – French and English.

For a writer as technically minded as Beckett, the attraction of Stein's work is clear, if one lays aside the politics of making such a connection given his ties to the Joyce circle: Stein wrote in an English devoid of the styles, affectations or intertextual practices of that same literary tradition. Stein also wrote in an English that in no way mimicked or manifested the particular stylistic affectations of Joyce; whatever one might say about Stein's work, is it decidedly not Joycean. Capable of subverting and sabotaging the structures of the English language from within the confines of that same language, Stein's unique idiolectic English represented a level of technical achievement Beckett had not yet achieved in his prose of the late 1930s, and so her appearance at a key juncture in the 1937 letter to Kaun is telling.

Despite the various interpretative approaches as to why Beckett adopted a bilingual writing praxis, his status as a bilingual writer is by now firmly established.[14] Beckett was not bilingual from birth, but became bilingual through determined and sustained effort; a facet of his bilingualism noted by both Montini (2007, 129) and Beer (1994, 214). While Beer notes that '[Beckett] made himself bilingual' (1994, 214), Stein was multilingual from early infancy.[15] Born into a first-generation German-speaking family who left America for Vienna when Stein was only eight months old, she grew up speaking German before being schooled in French after her family relocated to Paris when she was four. English was, in fact, Stein's third language, and she began to be systematically schooled in it only upon her return to America from Europe in September 1879 ('New York Passenger Lists, 1820–1891'). As Stein herself puts it in *Wars I Have Seen*, 'I was five years old when we came back to America having known Austrians Germans and French French, and now American English' (1984, 11). Studies of her undergraduate workbooks indicate she was not fully fluent until her early twenties, and Stein made similar errors relating to English grammar in college prose exercises to those Beckett made in his German prose of the 1930s (Wineapple, 2008, 15, 424n).

Stein carried many of the associated traits of her multilingual schooling through to her adult writing career, and her apparent difficulty in establishing a space for herself within the English language is palpable throughout her essays and lectures of the 1930s. In 'What Is English Literature' Stein makes explicit her belief that English literature – that is, the literature of England, a literature written in *British* English – is of little interest or relevance to her: 'There is then also the English people's history of their English literature but then after all that is their affair as far as I am concerned, as I am deeply concerned, it is none of my business' (Stein, 1998, 196). Instead, from *The Making of Americans* on, Stein discards aspects of anglophone orthography in favour of a hybridised bilingual style, incorporating francophone orthography into English prose and moving between capitalised and non-capitalised terms according to standard French style for proper nouns and adjectives, as seen in the following passage: 'They

---

[14] See Astbury (2001), Beer (1985, 1994), Cohn (1961, 1962, 95–113), Connor (1989), Federman (1987), Fitch (1988), Montini (2007), Mooney (2010, 2011), Sardin-Damestoy (2002), Scheiner (2013), Slote (2011, 2015), Stacey (2013, 2018) and Taylor-Batty (2013).

[15] References to this have been made in all major biographies of Stein. See Hobhouse (1975, 5), Satiat (2010, 22) and Wineapple (2008, 15, 424n).

were american [*sic*], they did not need french and german [*sic*]' (1995, 240). The iteration of 'American' in the previous example – 'they were american [*sic*]' – is noteworthy in that, following French capitalisation rules, if read as an adjective, the term should be left uncapitalised, but if read as a proper noun – also possible in this scenario – the term should be capitalised. Thus Stein, using English, manages to concoct a scenario wherein her francophone orthography in English treads a tenuous line between correct and incorrect, a masterly example of orthographically induced semantic tearing in action. Later, in *Paris, France*, Stein appears to modify her orthographic practice to suit the country she is speaking of, with 'the french [*sic*]' referred to using (incorrect) French orthography[16] and 'the English' using English: 'I like the word pastime as the french [*sic*] use it, it sounds so like the English word and yet the french [*sic*] make it so completely their own' (2003, 33).

In *The Autobiography of Alice B. Toklas*, this practice is explained in a manner that makes explicit the bilingual nature of Stein's aesthetics and practice as a writer: 'She [Stein] is passionately addicted to what the french [*sic*] call métier and she contends that one can only have one métier as one can only have one language. Her métier is writing and her language is english [*sic*]' (2001, 85). Of specific interest is the final sentence – 'her métier is writing and her language is english [*sic*]' (85) – which succinctly demonstrates the hybrid-ised and complex nature of her orthographic style. Stein uses a French term to classify herself as an English-language writer, referring to her *métier* as English, but at the same time, she employs French orthography to relay that English is her chosen language; thus the French *métier* is classified as English while the 'english [*sic*]' is relayed in a distinctly francophone manner. In this context, much of Stein's seemingly endless capacity to question and subvert the rules of acceptable speech appears less the product of self-consciously adopted icono-clasm and more a practical querying brought about by her multilingual upbringing.

As the child of German-American first-generation immigrants, who spent much of her early childhood in a non-anglophone environment, she maintained a strong sense that there was always more than one way to say something, together with an awareness that grammars varied not just from language to language, but from dialect to dialect. Stein's upbringing ensured she was aware of the existence of alternate expressions for every term used ('There are differ-ent ways of making of, of course' (Stein, 1975, 134)). As a proficient speaker of several languages, Stein had an apparently innate scepticism – 'a doubt a day' (48) – of the idea that there could only ever exist one way to say something.

---

[16] However, as a proper noun, 'the french' would be capitalised in French as 'Les Français'.

Raymond Federman makes the same observation in relation to Beckett: 'One can indeed wonder how often in the process of translating himself Beckett had to confront the *poverty* of certain French and English words in comparison with their equivalent in the other language' (1987, 11; emphasis in original). It is without question that the emergent and most coherent early articulations of what were to become Beckett's signature aesthetics of language were not only made in relation to writing in a language other than English, but were *articulated in* a language other than English. Moreover, they were concerned with importing the defamiliarisation felt while working in these other languages into a unilingual scenario involving Beckett's first language, English, with a view to making this language similarly strange from itself.

In *Samuel Beckett's Library*, Van Hulle and Nixon problematise the critical presumption that Beckett 'read Mauthner first to come up with the idea of comparing Gertrude Stein and James Joyce's diverging writing methods to Nominalism and Realism' by observing how, 'six days before he wrote the letter to Kaun, he told Thomas MacGreevy that he was reading "Schopenhauer on women"' (Van Hulle and Nixon, 2013, 145). This text, held as it is in the essay collection *Sämmtliche Werke*, 'is surrounded by essays on language and writing, books and reading, noise and silence. In particular chapter 25 ("Ueber Sprache und Worte", only two chapters before the essay on women) is almost certain to have drawn the attention of [the] young writer' (145).

The potential for a lack of connection with Mauthner prior to Beckett's decision to place Stein and Joyce in counterpoint at the centre of the 1937 letter to Kaun and his famous 'poetical statement on logoclasm' (Van Hulle and Nixon, 2013, 145) is important because, irrespective of the potential for a Schopenhauerian reading trace, it further strengthens the extent of the connection Beckett establishes between nominalism, nominalistic irony and Stein. Furthermore, it shows Beckett (whether he was aware of the fact or not) turning to naturally bilingual and polylingual writers like Stein or Mauthner and finding in their writing something he wished to emulate in his own, something that, in his case, could be acquired only through considerable effort. This is a facet Taylor-Batty also extrapolates when she suggests 'Mauthner's radical linguistic scepticism might itself be related not only to his own complex linguistic heritage [...] but to the methods of language teaching to which he was subjected' (2013, 156).

Van Hulle and Nixon's contention is particularly interesting when read in tandem with an insightful observation made by Knowlson in *Images of Beckett*. Knowlson suggests that Beckett began to compose in French 'not [...] out of a desire for greater clarity', but rather 'to attain an art in which, referring to

Gertrude Stein, the "texture of language has become porous"' (2003, 37). In introducing this quote from Knowlson, I am not seeking to mark Beckett's transition to composing in French as an event that was catalysed solely by his readings of Stein, but rather to suggest that Stein, and Stein's logographs in particular, played an integral role in Beckett's evasion of the 'grammar[s] and style[s]' (Beckett, 2009c, 518) of the English language. As has been seen in the preceding sections, Beckett's adoption of an aesthetic praxis that sees him engage in acts of renarration akin – if not identical – in their technical execution to those found in Stein, induces the very porosity Knowlson speaks of.

Cordingley and Montini situate 'Beckett's bilingual writing' in 'contrast with Joyce's multilingualism, which challenges and modifies "standard" English by accommodating foreign idioms' (2015, 10). '[Joyce's] multilingual practices', they assert, 'generate a liminal space between languages' (10). Yet Stein's work also challenges and modifies standard English, and it does so without the overt introduction of foreign idioms and without an excessive reliance on intertextuality. While Beckett's move between English and French is obvious by virtue of the different nature of the languages, Stein manages to make her prose strange without adopting the polyglot style of Joyce or indeed the mature bilingual praxis of Beckett. This fact is of particular relevance to the semantically and syntactically atypical modifications seen throughout *Watt*, a text Montini contends is of particular import within the bilingual oeuvre as the first major Beckett text wherein 'l'anglais et le français commencent à interagir [English and French begin to interact]' (2007, 154):

> Cette interaction, où l'anglais annonce la version française et où le français complète le texte anglais, grâce à l'explicitation par l'autre langue de la technique sous-jacente aux choix de certains mors; est caractéristique de beaucoup de versions bilingues de Beckett. (160)

> [This interaction, where the English announces the French version and where the French completes the English text, thanks to the explanation provided by the other language of the technique underlying the choice of certain bits, is characteristic of a lot of Beckett's bilingual versions.]

Mooney similarly classifies *Watt* as a 'tenuous English which leans perceptibly and disconcertingly towards French' (2011, 75). Beer refers to it as a text that marks 'a point of extreme bilingual tension' but one that also 'begins an exploration of English which continues, hidden and exposed, right through to *Worstward Ho*' (1994, 213). As was argued throughout Sections 3 and 4, the renarrative processes identifiable in *Watt* and Beckett's later fictions have definite precursors in the 'simplier' (Stein, 1975, 147) writings of Stein.

Watt certainly contains what Montini classifies as 'les germes du bilinguisme [the germs of bilingualism]' (2007, 23), not only in relation to the bilingual intertexts outlined throughout her study, but in the form of a more lexically conservative understanding of bilingual writing as a writing that incorporates or combines more than one language, what Slote refers to as 'an English inflected by French' (2015, 118). Mooney sees *Watt* as 'a form of farewell to English [...] which is characterised by the deformation of English away from its usual syntactical forms' (2010, 201) and further contends that *Watt* is 'a text which itself reads like a work of faulty machine-generated translation' (2011, 2). Montini similarly suggests that the language of *Watt* is of interest from a bilingual perspective because it has been in some way translated by the character/narrator 'Sam' into a language familiar to the reader. The character of Sam 'traduit et trahit [translates and betrays]' (Montini, 2011, 2) the stories Watt recounted to him, rendering them intelligible by rendering them into a language that is readable.

Watt, Montini argues, in contrast, 'ne peut faire référence qu'à son système intérieur, système qui, privé du langage [...] se révèle tellement chaotique qu'il est incompréhensible aux autres [can only make reference to his inner system, a system which, deprived of language [...] is so chaotic as to be incomprehensible to others]' (2011, 143). Though less concerned with the evolution of the Beckettian narrator, Mooney makes a similar connection:

> What is said, or heard, or repeated, appears to need to be interpreted or translated as if from an alien source; speakers draw attention to their own foreignisms, linguistic oddities, and mispronunciations [...] deictically making language visible both *as* language and as *a language*. (2011, 2–3; emphasis in original)

The critical contention, then, seems to be that *Watt* marks a definite stylistic progression away from the English language, but one that is largely enacted through the English language. To this end, Montini later asserts that '[Sam] n'est plus simplement le narrateur du roman, il est aussi l'interprète, le traducteur de Watt et son *créateur* [[Sam] is not simply the narrator of the book, he is also the interpreter, the translator of Watt and his *creator*]' (2011, 148; emphasis in original).

In *Watt*, as Montini notes, we are provided with the first example of a Beckettian narrator narrating (translating, rewriting) the narrative of another so as to make their incomprehensible narrative a bit more comprehensible for the reader. Throughout many of Stein's texts we are presented with passages equivalent in their esotericism to the Watt narrative, albeit without the aid of Sam's narratorial translations, imperfect and half-heard though they may be (Beckett, 2009f, 144). Certain of Stein's more esoteric texts can therefore be considered as displaying a narrative that is pre-translation and devoid of any aids that might enhance their comprehensibility. Unlike Beckett, who develops a particular type of narrating (and narrated) narrator in the form of Sam, Stein steadfastly refuses to provide the semantic 'keys' to unlock or make wholly unambiguous her writings. Commenting on her line 'rose is a rose is a rose is a rose', Stein is articulate in her awareness that her prose style does not accord to standard English dialect, and she appears committed to the obfuscation this engenders: 'Now I don't want to put too much emphasis on that line, because it's just one line in a longer poem. [. . .] I'm no fool. I know that in daily life we don't go around saying " . . . is a . . . is a . . . is a . . . ."' (2004, 7). Rather, she states, these peculiar syntactic patterns and atypical semantic connections are adopted out of a dissatisfaction with received language, a language Stein feels has lost 'the excitingness [*sic*] of pure being' and is now composed of 'wornout [*sic*] [. . .] stale literary words' (7). Much like Beckett, these linguistic and syntactic manipulations are adopted so as to enact an attack on the representative capacity of language, discrediting the mimetic capacity of language by drawing consistent attention to language *as language*, as an arbitrary and ill-functioning representative medium.

Montini's detailed delineation of the various interactions between Beckett's English and French texts sees her forward a thesis regarding 'la co-présence des deux langues dans chaque texte [the co-presence of two languages in every text]' (2007, 153). For Montini, the interactions between the two versions of a given text across the languages of English and French, or vice versa, the intertextual vicissitudes she identifies between the English and French versions of each text is what is characteristically bilingual in Beckett. This is also the particular model of Beckettian bilingualism presented by Banfield, Mooney, Schneider and Beer. Indeed, throughout the majority of interpretations of Beckett's bilingual *œuvre*, bilingual writing is presented as a scenario wherein 'les deux langues qu'on peut mieux les déchiffrer' [we can better decipher them [the bilingual versions] with both languages]' (160).

This understanding of bilingual writing or a bilingual poetics would be more accurately classified as bilingual intertext as opposed to bilingual writing proper. In the texts that comprise Beckett's bilingual oeuvre, a solution of sorts in the form of a satisfactory semantic description is, if not provided by means of intertext between the versions, then at least gestured towards by some aspect of the intertextual trafficking between the two texts (between the English or the French); what Banfield identifies as 'cross-lingual connections' (1994, 218). As Slote puts it, 'rather than exist in either the English and/or French versions, Beckett's texts exist *between* the French and English versions' (2011, 205; emphasis in original), even if, as Mooney observes, this space is a 'quasi-Proustian textual flickering between widely divergent moments in time' (2010, 199). As such, this sees an author-specific variety of bilingual intertext wherein the intertext is confined to only two texts,[17] or two texts that are versions of each other. It can be considered a minimal or greatly restricted variant of the 'monolingual polyglot' writings Montini classifies as characteristic of Beckett's pre-1937 work (2007, 33). Rather than collate an abundance of polylingual intertextual references within the confines of a single text (as Beckett does throughout *Dream*, for example), specific and nuanced intertextual references are codified between two texts that are versions of each other in two different languages; with the polylingual references themselves largely confined to two (bi-) languages (lingua) that constitute the author's first and second languages. These intratextual bilingual interactions are spread between the two versions, creating a complex, but nonetheless largely traceable bilingual pairing.

Stein's writings proffer no such inter- or intratextual pairings or solutions. Just as her logographs in *Tender Buttons* and elsewhere refuse to provide a clear passage of semantic reconciliation between term and description, her writing throughout texts such as *The Making of Americans* and *How to Write* inhibits even the most determined efforts to 'make sense' of her prose. In doing so, Stein denies the reader access to the explanations behind the esoteric and atypical semantics and syntaxes infused throughout the regular English prose of her writings. While not conducted in a bilingual English of the sort Montini proposed in her categorisation of Beckett's *Watt* as a bilingual Anglophonic text, Stein rather presents a version of English that incorporates non-standard syntactic patterns, phrasal formulations and semantic associations, a poly- or mixed-dialectical English wherein the atypical semantic connections established between certain words remain particular to the author – in short, an author-specific idiolect that merges standard English with idiolectic phraseology and private semantic connections.

This primarily involves the use and manipulation of a single (mono-) language (lingua), but is nevertheless distinct from Montini's 'monolongual polyglottism' because it:

(i) involves a form of code-switching that is dialectical and esoteric in that the alternate semantic terms are neither codified nor consistent; and

(ii) involves manipulations that are syntactically atypical in standard English.

---

[17] This is an author-specific simplification of the intra- and intertextual process, one that, for the purpose of this Element, excluded the manifold other intertextual or 'new cultural field' references Schneider notes Beckett encodes into each version 'so that it may resonate for the new reader', what she later refers to as 'Beckett's practice of cultural transposition' (2013, 374–5, 377).

That which is incorporated into the writings to make the language strange from itself comes in the form of the uniquely Steinian syntactic aberrations that bring about semantically atypical word associations, or, alternatively, semantic aberrations that hint at or instigate syntactic dysfunction that cannot be rectified or made determinate. These associations are not relayed through the incorporation of terms that can be identified as belonging to a non-English lexicon, nor through the pairing of that text, word or passage with an alternate, rewritten or translated text, word or passage in another language, as in the case of Beckett's bilingual oeuvre.

Tender Buttons saw Stein produce what Joshua Schuster refers to as 'an extraordinary new grammar' (2011), one that was achieved on a semantic, lexical and syntactic level. Prior to this, in *The Making of Americans* Stein developed an equally extraordinary new syntax of elaborate and exhaustive permutations. The inter-clausal syntactic manipulations employed by the authors in texts such as *Watt* and *The Making of Americans* saw them similarly attempt to subvert normative English grammars, breaking the English language up in arbitrary ways. Instances of semantic sense or certitude last roughly for the period of a clause or phrase before a syntactic recalibration sees these values deferred or modified, or translated in phrase by phrase or clausal semantic recalibrations. This was an aesthetic Stein pursued in a unilingual format but one that was multi-dialectical and, to borrow Montini's terminology, effectively saw Stein writing in an author-specific bilingual English. While Beckett's bilingual English as delineated by Montini involves the gradual introduction of francophone assonances into English prose, Beckett's writing throughout *Watt* also sees him employ techniques identical to those of Stein.

Just as in Stein's 'rose is a rose is a rose is a rose', linguistic arbitrariness is similarly highlighted throughout *Watt*, as Montini makes explicit: 'L'écriture de *Watt* vise plutôt à mettre à nu l'impossibilité d'une correspondance entre mots et choses et l'absurdité d'utiliser le langue comme s'il représentait quelque chose de réel [*Watt*'s writing aims rather to expose the impossibility of a correspondence between words and things and the absurdity of using language as if it is representing something real]' (2007, 150). Montini's argument here accords with one of the two main techniques that are an implicit aspect of both authors' renarrative styles, namely the use of syntax to highlight semantic arbitrariness. Montini classifies Watt as 'le deuxième roman du *bilinguisme à dominance anglophone*, que le mécanisme frayant le chemin vers le "dévoilement du langue" (souvenons-nous de la lettre à Axel Kaun) [the second novel of a *predominantly English bilingualism*, the mechanism spawning the path towards the "unveiling of language" (remembering the letter to Axel Kaun)]' (96; emphasis in original).

Further still, Montini observes 'que la langue anglaise est portée à l'extrême et marque pour cela un point de non retour [the English language is taken to an extreme and therefore marks a point of no return]' (97). That Stein played a key role in facilitating this point of no return, which ultimately became respect for Beckett's relationship with the English language, should, by now, be manifestly evident. Beckett identified Stein's logography as a necessary stage 'on the road towards this, for me, very desirable literature of the non-word' (Beckett, 2009c, 520). For Beckett, this nominal logography ultimately evolved beyond a monolingual scenario with the splitting of each of his works across two languages, creating two versions of every 'well-built phrase' (Beckett, 2009d, 29) and inducing intertextual porosities of the kind Stein was content to facilitate solely within the English language.

Watt's speech throughout his exchanges with Sam, to be returned to in Section 7, could even be considered logographic, especially if we consider Mooney's contention that 'The novel moves between the poles of the intricately reversed, cryptic idiolect Watt speaks [. . .] and which the narrator, Sam, has to decipher or translate, and, on the other hand, a nostalgia for "the old words, the old credentials"' (Mooney, 2010, 201). Indeed, the syntactic arrangements of the passages throughout the Watt/Sam exchange do not accord with standard English word order, and Chris Ackerley consistently refers to these passages as ones that 'might' be translated/translatable, usefully elucidating each of these lexically convoluted passages with a passage in standard English that represents what 'a "translation" might read' (2010, 156). Watt's speech is thus logographic in a manner similar to that of Stein's *Tender Button*, presenting words in other words. They are English language logographs, or exercises in logography. Yet, while Beckett (via his translator/narrator Sam) provides the reader with a clear key or route to making the nonsensical sensible, Stein does not provide this for her readers throughout *Tender Buttons* or elsewhere.

If 1937 marked the turning point for Beckett away from the polyglot writings of Joyce and towards a bilingual anglophone writing, then *Watt* sees Beckett address the nominalistic irony he references in 1937 and move beyond it, precisely through the development of the narrator Montini identifies as an integral facet of the Sam/Watt interchange. It was in these specific passages of *Watt* that Beckett took on and transcended the nominalistic irony or logography he saw as a facet (but an integral facet nonetheless) of his progression towards a 'literature of the non-word' (Beckett, 2009c, 520). Stein's logographs, together with her lengthy and relentless renarrations, facilitated Beckett's crafting of an aesthetics that transcended the limitations posed by such 'grammar bound' (Stein, 1975, 65), nominally focussed practices.

Beckett's more orthodox bilingualism serves the same purpose as Stein's partly esoteric multi-dialectical writing in that it similarly 'denies the reader access to any unified or originary surface of interpretation, consciousness, or meaning' (Mooney, 2010, 199). Ultimately, both achieve what Mooney describes as 'the blurring of boundaries by the existence of two imperfectly matched versions of most texts, among which the reader can find no clear sense of the definitive or authoritative, [an effect that] renders the idea of the individual work oddly porous' (197). Whereas Beckett's work is split between two texts, Stein's remains within a single body, keeping core aspects of the semantic assonances from her readers.

6 'Waste No More Time Trying to Get It Right': Beckett and Stein's 'Fidelity to Failure'[18]

Stein, unlike Joyce, did not purport all errors to be deliberate and the work or by-product of genius. Yet, many of the examples of error I will presently discuss appear particularly suited to the context within which they appear throughout her narratives. Taken together, they make for a persuasive argument that Stein not so much took advantage of errors when they occurred in her writings, seeing them perhaps as an opportunistic 'portal of discovery' (Joyce, 2007, 9.156.228–9), but rather saw the promotion of certain semantic or syntactic errors throughout her texts as opportunities to create increasingly inexact narratives, adopting a mode of pejorative writing directly analogous to Beckett's own pejorative late prose style. Approaching *The Making of Americans* from the perspective of the author's intentions for it to be a 'history of every one who ever was or is or will be living' (Stein, 1995, 176) for example, suggests that grammatical inexactitude and error are necessary – if not essential – aspects of Stein's vast schema of peoples. A 'completer' (330) one in this 'history of all of the kinds of them and of each one of all the millions of each kindof [*sic*] them' (177) would naturally incorporate error, with these errors frequently taking the form of semantic and syntactic aberrations that serve to 'make a completer [*sic*] one of that one' (330) the narrator is currently in the process of describing.

Beyond the necessary presence of a degree of error in this history of all peoples, Stein appears to have embraced an aesthetic credo that places error and the associated act of failing (particularly of intentional failure) on a similar par with correctness, exactitude and accuracy. In other words, Stein was equally interested in getting it wrong as in getting it right, a sentiment encapsulated in the following line from *How to Write*: 'When I have not been right there must be something wrong' (Stein, 1995, 573), noted previously. Acknowledging the existence of this 'something' and attempting to further articulate it, irrespective

---

[18] Beckett, 2009e, 42; 2001, 145.

of its morphological status as 'right' or 'wrong' in the context of acceptable English grammar, represents as valid an enterprise for Stein as the pursuit of the 'right'. Beckett's aesthetics of failure, epitomised in his statement regarding a 'fidelity to failure' (Beckett, 2001, 145) in *Three Dialogues* and enacted in his post-1937 writings, is more directly compatible with Stein's similar attitude to error in her writings, than with the Joycean conception of error as a 'portal of discovery' (Joyce, 2007, 9.156.228–9).

We see regular examples of apparently deliberate syntactic or semantic errors throughout Stein's prose writings, from early works such as *The Making of Americans* through to later writings such as 'Enface' or 'Pfoems pritten on Pfances of George Hugnet' (Stein, 1996, 301). Beckett identifies the subversive potential of error through the incorrect application of 'Grammar and style!' (Beckett, 2009c, 518) in his letter to Kaun in 1937 when he notes that the aesthetics he is leaning towards have thus far been achieved only by accident while writing in German – that is, working in a language other than English, a tertiary language he was not at the time fluent in. When making such (unintentional) errors he undermines the stand-ard dialect he is attempting to emulate in his German writing. His errors in German thus qualify as subversions to the set rules of the German language, but they are subversions made in ignorance and Beckett desires to do more than enact linguistic porosity through morphological ignorance. Instead, he wishes to knowingly subvert his own language (at the time, English). To achieve the same or similar effects through deliberate action would thus involve writing in incorrect English, employing the grammars of the English language against the language system itself. This action is remarkably proximate, if not aesthetically identical, to Stein's similar harnessing of the subversive potential of error through certain technical and stylistic mechan-isms adopted in her literary writings, and to the technical praxis of renarra-tion as outlined throughout the preceding sections of this Element.

English was Stein's third language, and while, as noted earlier, Stein's English remained imperfect throughout her teens and into her early twenties (Wineapple, 2008, 15, 424n), the famed account of her publishing house's reaction upon reading her draft of *Three Lives* occurred when her command of English was fluent:

> One day some one knocked at the door and a very nice very american [*sic*] young man asked if he might speak to Miss Stein. [. . .] He said, I have come at the request of the Grafton Press. [. . .] You see, he said, slightly hesitant, the director of the Grafton Press is under the impression that perhaps your knowledge of english [*sic*]. [. . .] perhaps you have not had much experience in writing. (Stein, 2001, 76)

Stein's response, as relayed in *The Autobiography of Alice B. Toklas*, was to firmly assert the intentionality behind her prose style: 'I [Stein] will write to the director and you might as well tell him also that everything that is written in the manuscript is written with the intention of it being so written and all he has to do is print it and I will take the responsibility' (76).

The Making of Americans sees Stein employ more elaborate repetitious formulae to those seen throughout *Three Lives* that so concerned her first publisher. As we have seen in Sections 3 and 4, these syntactic manipulations force words into unusual or inaccurate declensions, creating phrases and sentences whose closest comparison might be found in the expressions of a non-native, non-fluent speaker.

Rather than seeking to be as accurate as possible, in the knowledge that linguistic expression is a fundamentally unsatisfactory medium where all is inaccurate and all representation is ill-represented, these deliberate incorporations of error and the outright pursuit of error bring about a sort of reverse procedure to the traditional understanding of literary representation as mimetic. Instead, it creates a scenario wherein both Beckett and Stein can be said to mine inaccuracies in the search for the 'best worse' (Beckett, 2009a, 95), as Beckett puts it in *Worstward Ho*, a conscious and deliberate de-mimeticising of language. Both authors appear to use error to create a more exact inexactitude, one created in the certainty that exactitude itself is unobtainable. To this end we might now return to the third of Beckett's *Three Dialogues*, discussed in Section 2, which sees the dialoguer – 'B ' – bring up the issue of a 'fidelity to failure, a new occasion, a new term of relation, and of the act which, unable to act, obliged to act' (2001, 145). The third dialogue relates to the visual artist Bram van Velde and so, much like the first dialogue on Pierre Tal Coat, it cannot be too much divorced from its initial context. Yet at the same time, this recognition on Beckett's part of an artist endeavouring to fail as opposed to succeed hints again at what it was about Stein's writings that so attracted him in 1937 when, as he notes, she displayed a distinct disinterest in 'the solution of the problem', instead presenting it as 'of very secondary interest' (Beckett, 2009c, 519).

Beckett and Stein's tendency to employ neologisms that do not read as clever, lexically inventive new word forms, but rather as overtly simplified language – what Van Hulle and Weller classify as 'pejoration' (2014, 209) – language that could in fact be considered lexically uninventive to the point of being grammatically incorrect, stands in contrast to Joyce's. By extension, it stands in contrast with the more elaborate neologisms found throughout Beckett's early works, which displayed strong imitative tendencies towards Joyce. Beckett and Stein's respective attitudes to error – and in particular their shared use of distinctive (and distinctively non-Joycean) neologisms – can be seen as a direct bridge through which we can segue from the Beckett of 1937 – who aspired to certain aesthetics similar to those Stein had already achieved – and his later writings wherein these once proposed aesthetics have been actualised; where the 'worser worst' (Beckett, 2009a, 95) is manifestly evident, and evident across writings that span two languages.

As mentioned earlier in this Element, Beckett notes in the van Velde dialogue that van Velde 'is the first to admit that to be an artist is to fail, as no other dare fail, that failure is his world' (Beckett, 2001, 145). In a similar vein, Stein considered *Tender Buttons* to have 'as much failure as success in it' (Stein, 1971, 29–30), and while this suggests a capacity on her part to identify failure when it occurs in her work, her classification of the text as part failure appears to be specific to the aesthetic aims of the piece as an attempt to do nothing less than 'replac[e] the noun' (Stein, 2004, 136). In contrast, the following passage from *The Making of Americans* sees Stein not only express satisfaction with being occasionally incorrect, but go so far as to explicitly pursue error:

> I have always been very interested in seeing how very wrong I can be when I am telling about any one how they are going to be living from day to day in their living [. . .] and always then I want to be mistaken I want to make mistakes so that I can see something in them which makes of that one a more complete one, always then I want to be feeling more certain of all the variations that makes some one so very much like some one really different from that one. (Stein, 1995, 538)

This explicit embracing of error in the form of 'want[ing] to be mistaken' should serve to correct Beckett's assertion about van Velde. As David Lodge suggests, if the work is a failure, it is so 'because it attempts something that violates the very essence of her medium, language: the combination axis of language cannot be so brutally dislocated without defeating the system's inherently communicative function. *Tender Buttons* is a feat of *de*-creation (1977, 154).

Having established the compatible nature of Beckett and Stein's aesthetics of failure, error or inexactitude, the following passages will display and contrast concrete examples from their prose texts that illustrate the extensive comparability of their approach to the deliberate promotion of error throughout their writings, especially their similarly atypical use of the suffix.

The supposedly francophone overtones of the title of Stein's *Tender Buttons* are regularly relayed in critical analyses of the text, most explicitly by Perloff, who sees the title as a 'kind of Dada joke for, by definition, buttons are not tender. [. . .] It has been suggested that Gertrude Stein is referring to buds (the French *tendre boutons*) or to nipples' (1999, 99). Perloff is not the first to make a connection between the English *Tender Buttons* and its French homophone. Lodge writes that the title may be a metaphor for nipples because 'buttons cannot literally be tender' (1977, 153). Earlier still, Paul Padgette, in a 1971 letter to the *New York Review of Books*, claims 'the title *Tender Buttons*, of course, refers to a woman's nipples' (Padgette, 1971). Yet there are limits to the usefulness of the French phonemic pun, which serves mainly as a facile metaphor for Stein's treatment of language throughout the text. Reading the title as metaphor encourages readings such as Perloff's own, wherein she notes that 'perhaps the best way to take the title is simply as an indication that the text itself will emphasise metamorphosis: hard objects become soft, wet objects dry up, persons turn into objects, buttons sprout before our eyes' (1999, 99).

The Germanic nature of the title is more interesting, with *Tender Buttons* forming a sort of compound word for Stein, one she clearly contrived out of necessity, finding no suitable alternative in English. It is also an aspect of the text that, to my knowledge, has received little or no attention, despite the fact that during the years 1912–14, Stein's command of German (her first language) would have been as advanced, if not more advanced, than her grasp of French. With this in mind, the text's title, *Tender Buttons*, can be presented as an anglicised version of the Germanic *komposita*, the forming of compound words out of two otherwise unrelated terms. This sees Stein continuing the tendency to subject the English language to Germanic syntaxes or certain idiosyncrasies of German grammar that did not have a counterpart in English, as is manifestly evident throughout *The Making of Americans*. Indeed, it is a development on the polylingual merging seen throughout *The Making of Americans* because it sees Stein transcend the limits of strictly Germanic or English syntaxes and instead enact a sort of syntactic code-switching between standard English or German, employing a curious non-standard alternative dialect that seemed unique to its author, what Susan Gubar classified as 'Steinese' (2000, 40).

This places Stein in a complementary position with respect to Beckett's similar use of *komposita* throughout his early writings. Nixon, commenting on the 'generally irreverent tone of *Dream of Fair to Middling Women*', observes that this irreverence is 'compounded by Beckett's mocking attitude towards the German language and the pedantry it so often expresses. This is particularly evident in the fun Beckett has with compound nouns, a German speciality, when coming up with names' (2011, 10). Nixon presents Beckett's adoption of *komposita* as particularly reflective of certain negative aspects of Beckett's early prose style, as indeed it was. More important, however, is their shared tendency to import syntaxes or attributes of a foreign language onto their work in English. This not only anticipates Beckett's later switch to preferring the unusual 'logographs' of Stein to the work of Joyce, but suggests that both authors were using their polylinguistic skills to merge and mutate that which could be considered standard in English prose.

While Nixon ties Beckett's use of *komposita* to *Dream of Fair to Middling Women*, it is not unreasonable to suggest that this action continued far beyond this early work, and in fact became a recurrent feature of Beckett's mature prose style, albeit in a subtler format than the showy compound terms found throughout *Dream*. This takes effect largely through Beckett's adoption of the suffix '-er' in conjunction with terms that do not normally take the '-er' suffix, an approach also particularly noticeable in the case of Stein's *Tender Buttons*. In grafting suffixes on to supposedly incompatible terms, Stein was transgressing the syntax of standard English, employing a pejorative praxis that merits comparisons with the technique of *komposita*: she made new words out of old terms, or parts of old terms. Stein's frequent addition of the '-er' suffix to terms that are not just incompatible semantically, but incompatible functionally too (making adjectives function as verbs, and so on) lends the syntax a somewhat Germanic feel that mirrors (or, more correctly, anticipates) Beckett's own use of the suffix in association with terms that do not take the '-er' suffix in normative English dialect.

The suffixation of words that do not comply with the morphemes used sees both authors import their own endings and thus impose their own meanings (or non-meanings) onto various terms with minimal interference to the word unit itself, for, as Beckett's narrator makes clear in 'Texts for Nothing VIII', without an ending, a word has no meaning 'like a single endless word and therefore meaningless, for it's the end gives meaning to words' (2009e, 33). The '-er' suffix thus plays an integral role in the deliberate enticing of error into their narrative because it sees both authors focus on the manipulation of grammatical modifiers as a means of subverting that which is considered standard or normative within English dialect and, by means of a renarration that appends a suffix, presenting the word as semantically deviant. The suffix plays an important role in both the diminution and expansion of descriptive attributes in grammar. In the following examples from texts by both authors, this attributive tendency is co-opted to suggest a specificity that is belied by the fact that the words themselves break new ground by becoming new versions of their head term, the unsuffixed root term that has been modified.

Stein is particularly partial to incorporating the '-er' suffix into her writings. Often the appearance of an aberrational use of the suffix is preceded, as it is in the following example, by an orthodox employment of same: 'Anyway, to be older and ageder' (Stein, 2014, 38). This accords with the tendency, noted previously, to surround an instance of semantic or syntactic diversity with correspondingly archetypal language so as to better emphasise the atypical modification taking place. Beckett also uses this junctured approach to the introduction of error, albeit in a reversed format, with the 'incorrect' term preceding the 'correctly' suffixed word: 'So Watt busied himself a little while, covering the lamp, less and less, more and more, with his hat, watching the ashes greyen, redden, greyen, redden, in the grate, of the range' (Beckett, 2009f, 30). A word such as 'distincter' (Stein, 2014, 13) in Stein's description of 'A Piece of Coffee' is directly analogous to Beckett's similar coining of the word 'greyen' (Beckett, 2009f, 30) here. In these grammars of 'the same sight slighter' (Stein, 2014, 13), objects are assigned a certain descriptive character-istic only for that to be tweaked throughout the minute grammatical renarration that is the addition of a suffix.

The following instance of suffixed modification, taken from *Tender Buttons*, is a nice example of cumulative repetitions that incite error through the addition of the '-er' suffix first to an indeterminate adjective/noun, and then to a noun: 'The sight of a reason, the same sight slighter, the sight of a simple negative answer, the same sore sounder, the intention of wishing, the same splendor [*sic*], the same furniture' (Stein, 2014, 13). First, the adjective 'slight', a term that has phonemic similarities with its associated noun/verb 'sight', is modified to read as 'slighter', a term that is indeed a slighter version of 'slight'. Syntactically, in the context of this passage, this term should function as an adjectival qualifier of 'sight', but the word itself is also capable of functioning as a noun and as a verb. This modification of 'slight' to 'slighter' alters the semantics of the term and renders it semantically incompatible with its surrounding modifiers. Reading the term as a noun is within the horizon of plausible interpretation – the noun 'slighter' refers to 'one who slights or disdains' (*OED*). But in the context of the phrase 'the same sight slighter', this makes little semantic sense unless it relates a truncated account of seeing this 'slighter' figure again, which is unlikely as the passage belongs to a paragraph supposedly describing 'A Piece of Coffee' (Stein, 2014, 13). The syntactic arrangement of this clause makes the modified term read as a semantic error, one that defers our capacity to make sense of what is being seen, of what (or who) is being slighted or considered a 'slighter'. In short, it hinders our capacity to make sense of the passage at all. With its iteration of 'the same sight slighter', the passage appears to have found a favoured pejorative format. It recurs as the grammatical template for three subsequent repetitions, two of which similarly adopt the '-er' suffix in precisely the same manner. Incorrectly appended or conspicuous suffixes occur in the line 'the same sore sounder' with 'the same' remaining 'the same' while the associated pairing 'sore sounder' presents a similarly semantically dubious portrait of a pained figure engaged in uttering sounds, a 'sore sounder' (*OED*). Employing the 'correct' phraseology throughout any of these previous passages is far from Stein's intention. The courting of error appears here, as elsewhere, altogether deliberate, brought about through the precise and skilful manipulation of syntax in tandem with semantically obscure terms, so as to fashion passages that are invariably difficult to resolve to any set meaning.

Beckett shows more variety than Stein in terms of the suffixes he adopts, though *How It Is* contains the following example of an '-er' suffix appended in a manner identical to Stein's discussed previously: 'resurrect an instant then leave for deader than before' (Beckett, 2009b, 95). In this instance, however, the surrounding modifiers further enhance the nonsensical nature of the passage as it is theoretically impossible for a figure, once dead, to be considered more dead than they had heretofore been. This presents a finite event as something that instead exists on a spectrum of varying levels of 'deadness'. The ontological impossibility of this is correspondingly indicated by the semantically inappropriate terms used to relay the event, namely what is biologically impossible is correspondingly relayed in a manner that is grammatically incorrect.

The use of neologisms in the work of both authors largely involves instances when the language gets worse (worser) as the narrative progresses; as the narrative progresses, the language regresses, reverting to syntactically inelegant, grammatically incorrect phrases that induce a corresponding and discernable semantic uncertainty. In this way, then, it is fair to argue that such tactical deployment of suffixes, when paired with appropriate (and by that I mean inappropriate or atypical) surrounding modifiers, are clear instances of both authors strategically employing grammatically derived strategies to incite semantic fissures or tears in 'the fabric of the language' (Beckett, 2009c, 519), again, the Steinian practice Beckett so wished to emulate in 1937.

7 Conclusion: 'Say It Simply. [. . .] Say It Simplier'[19]

What emerges throughout the course of this Element is the validity of positing Stein as a key influence on Beckett's developing aesthetics of language throughout the 1930s, of Stein as an integral stylistic touchstone against whom we can situate Beckett's aesthetics, and in particular, the emergence of an English creative praxis that made use of the technique of renarration as a deliberate method for inducing semantic and syntactic inconsistencies, indeterminacies, and – metaphorically speaking – *tears* in the veil or fabric of the English language (Beckett, 2009c, 518–19). This situates Beckett's nascent bilingual praxis and his 'literature of the non-word' (520) within a wider continuum of influence and stylistic comparability than his writings have thus far been exposed to. It repositions Stein as a central figure in the development of Beckett's aesthetics of language in particular, and it situates Beckett and Stein as two figures whose aesthetics and creative praxis display remarkable

---

[19] Stein, 1975, 147.

confluences that reward further study. It also works to redress the critical perception of Stein as a marginal or somewhat isolated figure whose work progressed 'by accident' (519) – a major figure in literary modernism whose esoteric writings have left many critics and readers at a loss in terms of establishing relatable connections (other than coterie-driven connections) to other key figures in the European modernist scene.

Both authors' explorations of the problems of language and their solutions to these problems as evident in their fictional writings appear remarkably coherent and compatible, rendering their aesthetics wholly confluential. Stein emerges as a key influential figure on the aesthetics of Beckett, whose early writings have continually been presented through the lens of Joyce. This Element has made clear that both authors employ deviant renarrations involving the minutiae of grammar to undo semantic stability both on a clausal level and on a larger scale. In addition to their shared adoption of semantic strategies of renarration that induce indeterminacy, antonymous and conflicting meanings, and deferred or asymptotic semantic certitude, their manipulations of syntax have similarly been revealed to play a major role in the displacing of semantic certainty in the English language. Stein has been shown to be particularly effective at enabling such nuanced instances of grammatically incorrect writings. This is a literary style that, while evident throughout certain of his early-to-mid period works (such as *Watt*), Beckett himself did not embrace outright until later, culminating in the 'best worse' (Beckett, 2009a, 103) of *Worstward Ho*. Nevertheless, that Beckett was making use of a deliberate renarrative technique involving grammatical manipulations that was similarly employed by Stein is manifestly evident.

The technique of renarration has been shown to display a number of recurrent characteristics when employed by both authors to facilitate acts of sabotage against the English grammar system. Stability of semantic meaning in one aspect of the statement or clause enables the introduction of semantic indeterminacy in the other. To enable semantic modification at least one aspect of the surrounding clause needs to retain stability as an anchoring device so that the reader can identify the grammatical indiscretion and register its effect on the narrative. Stein's use of conspicuous errors in particular relies on a series of near-identical repetitions and passages containing 'correct' terms, or 'correctly spelled' terms, if nothing else; these provide the counterpoint against which the deviations from standard spelling and semantic usage set themselves apart. Many of the examples discussed throughout this Element merit being read with Stein's concept of 'naive realism' (Stein, 1995, 445), as articulated throughout *The Making of Americans*, in mind. Similarly, her statement from *How to Write* that 'literalness is not deceptive it destroys similarity' (Stein, 1975, 70), noted in the

Introduction, can be seen to be in effect throughout their engagements with the renarration of major and minor grammatical modifiers, having precisely the effect Stein observes in that literal renarration serves to 'destroy' the renarrated terms' capacity to signify the otherwise usually semantically nuanced items they signify. Harnessing these instances of excessive literalness – 'naive realism' (Stein, 1995, 445) – through repetition with nuanced modifications is particularly effective in relation to lexical units that are themselves primarily (if not exclusively) vehicles for conveying nondescript lexical concepts or relations that exist only within the context of a literal linguistic construct, terms that function solely within the realm of grammar for which there is no set, concrete counterpart. While this Element was confined to covering the renarration of nouns, verbs and pronouns, the remarkable crossover between Beckett and Stein's renarrative praxes, the sheer similarity in their styles, continues in their respective engagement with conjunctions, determiners and prepositions.[20]

This Element introduces a major authorial connection into the field of Beckett studies in the form of Stein, Stein's influence on Beckett's aesthetics, and their role as confluential figures within literary modernism. The links between Beckett and Stein clearly go beyond the *might have been* or *perhaps* of Cohn and Knowlson, mentioned in the Introduction. Rather, this comparability can be delineated in an empirical, qualitative manner, with a remarkable proximity not only in their aesthetics of language, but in their stylistics. The result is a stylistic and aesthetic overlap so markedly extensive and a body of work so compatible that the connection between Beckett and Stein proves to be more than a mere convenient pairing. Rather, it situates Stein as a major confluential figure against which the aesthetics of Beckett can be better understood and contextualised, a figure whose writings are, as Beckett himself states in 1937, perhaps the closest contemporary counterpart to the aesthetics of language Beckett envisioned for himself throughout the 1930s and later realised in his mature writings.

While not altogether identical in terms of their practical output, their respective aesthetics of language appear, at times, almost identical in terms of the theoretical concepts they engage with. In the context of this comparative study, Stein emerges as a writer whose work epitomises the subversions of 'Grammar and style!' (Beckett, 2009c, 519) Beckett was looking to develop in his own work as declared in his letter to Kaun. This now-established connection will benefit from further research that expands its remit to include both writers' dramatic works – many of Stein's experiments with dramatic form merit

---

[20] See Nugent-Folan (2016) for a significantly more detailed study of Beckett and Stein's comparability across all grammatical modifiers.

immediate comparison with Beckett's later dramatic works – and their shared interest in the genre of film and cinema – Stein's 'Film: Deux Soeurs Qui ne Sont Pas Soeurs', published in *Revue Européene* in 1930 (Wilson, 1974, 131), demonstrates that Stein was experimenting with the medium, and doing so in French, at roughly the same time Beckett had significant access to the Paris-based periodicals and magazines through which he likely first encountered her writings. Indeed, it is even possible that Beckett's first encounter with Stein's work occurred in French, be that in the form of a French composition Stein herself authored (such as 'Film') or in the form of a translation, an altogether exciting prospect.[21]

One necessity for the recognition of 'abuse' of apropos language is a capacity on the part of the reader to set the writing in contrast against 'normal' or 'standardised' semantic contexts. In Beckett, by and large, prior to entering renarrations that enact modifications that could be considered 'abusive', the preceding and subsequent non-renarrated passages are relatively typical and consistent semantically. This is not always the case in Stein who, as I have stated, was less concerned with semantic consistencies, favouring instead a relentless assault against coherency, semantic surety and stability across the grammars of the English language. In neglecting to attend to the syntactic coherency of the sentence unit in favour of the 'logographs' (Beckett, 2009c, 519) Beckett identifies in his letter to Kaun, Stein develops an idiosyncratic, changeable, and author-specific idiolect that is exceedingly difficult, but as this Element has made clear, not impossible to parse. What further links Beckett and Stein is that their writings (irrespective, in Beckett's case, of whether these writings are conducted in English or in French) focus on encounters that, much like the inter- or polylingual writings of their contemporaries, are characterised by what Taylor-Batty refers to as 'misunderstanding, incomplete comprehension and distortion' (2013, 39).

Beckett and Stein also emerge as comparable and confluential because they are writers who made, what Fitch determines in the case of Beckett, 'the choice of a second acquired language over a first, native language' (1988, 8). In his introduction to Montini's *La bataille du soliloque*, Bruno Clément comments that while Montini's work on Beckett's bilingualism is the first of its kind, 'cette poétique ne se réduit pas à lui [this poetics is not confined to him]' (Clément, 2007, 15). Stein represents just such another writer whose work operated by means of a poetics of bilingualism. In contrast with Beckett, however, this bilingual methodology was pervasive throughout her career from early pieces through to the later works, and, in further contrast with Beckett, her work

---

[21] See Wilson (1974, 146–51) for details of Stein's book-length and journal publications in French.

remained predominantly of the kind Montini categorises as bilingually anglophonic (2007, 96). While the specificities of this anglophonic bilingualism vary between the two authors, this nevertheless situates Stein as a direct and immediate predecessor to the poetics of bilingualism – anglophonic or otherwise – Beckett develops from *Murphy* through to the complex lexical and phrasal renarrations of *Watt*.

In adopting and adapting the strategic and systematic techniques of semantic and syntactic estrangement seen throughout Stein's writings, Beckett was ultimately able to transcend the limitations of the English 'Grammar and style!' (Beckett, 2009c, 518) that impeded his aesthetic development throughout the 1930s, an act that was an integral factor in the development of his bilingual oeuvre. Whereas Joyce and his writing in the *Wake* can be considered an exemplary model of Montini's 'monolingual polyglot' (2007, 33) writing, Stein's work exists in stark stylistic opposition to this model. Resolutely anglophonic, resolutely monolingual, Stein nevertheless seemed to consider English *her* language, with the possessive determiner here of pivotal importance. As she puts it *The Autobiography of Alice B. Toklas*:

> One of the things that I have liked all these years [spent living in Paris] is to be surrounded by people who know no english [*sic*]. It has left me more intensely alone with my eyes and my english [*sic*]. I do not know if it would have been possible to have english [*sic*] be so all in all to me otherwise. [. . .] I like living with so very many people and being all alone with english [*sic*] and myself. (Stein, 2001, 77–8)

Montini underlines the importance of *Watt* as 'le premier roman écrit entièrement en France [the first novel written entirely in France]' (2007, 101), written in both geographic and linguistic exile: 'Le dernier roman en anglais de Beckett représente d'abord la coupure du cordon au sens littéral et métaphorique, précède a séparation de la langue maternelle [Beckett's last novel in English represents the cutting of the cord in both the literal and metaphorical sense, preceded a separation of the mother tongue]' (103). Stein too seems to have attached particular import to this similar geographic and linguistic estrangement in terms of the development of her own idiolectic variant of standard English. Indeed, Stein says as much in the excerpt just cited when she states 'I do not know if it would have been possible to have english [*sic*] be so all in all to me otherwise' (2001, 78). This geographic and linguistic exile facilitated her capacity to think of the English language as belonging 'all in all to me' (78), to develop a unique bilingual idiolect, and in the process, to transcend the habits of English 'Grammar and style!' (Beckett, 2009c, 518) that were so pertinent a problem to Beckett in and around the year 1937.

To conclude, then, Stein's work, and her very particular dialect of 'english [*sic*]' (Stein, 2001, 78), served as – and facilitated – an integral aesthetic pivot for Beckett, and this process was arguably serialised or dramatised lexically throughout the novel *Watt*. This can be seen most acutely in the text's exploration of the particulars of Watt's relationship with the English language, and in his unique and consistently changing idiolect. Like Stein, Watt's lexical output (his speech) seems to vary on an almost passage-by-passage level. Throughout *Tender Buttons*, for example, the prose pieces that accompany a quadruple repetition of the noun 'Chicken' each contain vastly different lexical content:

> Chicken
> Pheasant and chicken, chicken is a peculiar third.
>
> Chicken
> Alas a dirty word, alas a dirty third alas a dirty third, alas a dirty bird.
>
> Chicken
> Alas a doubt in case of more go to say what it is cress. What is it. Mean. Potatoe [*sic*]. Loaves.
>
> Chicken
> Stick stick call then, stick stick sticking, sticking with a chicken. sticking in a extra [*sic*] succession, sticking in. (Stein, 2014, 54–5)

This successively changing content is no different to Watt's paragraph by paragraph altering of the lexical arrangement of his speech output, or indeed from Sam's concordantly changing translations of Watt's ever-changing narratives:

> *Day of most, night of part, Knott with now. Now till up, little seen sooh, little heard so oh. Night till morning frim. Heard I this, saw I this then what. Thing quiet, dim. Ears, eyes, failing now also. Hush in, mist in, moved I so.* [. . .]
>
> *Ot bro, lap rulb, krad klub. Ot murd, wol fup, wol fup. Ot nicks, sorg sam, sorg sam. Ot lems, lats lems, lats lems. Ot gnut, trat stews, trat stews* [*sic*]. (Beckett, 2009f, 142–3; emphasis in original)

They are both, then, figures that, like the 'crazy mathematician' (Beckett, 2009c, 520) of the 1937 Kaun letter, prioritise process over result, figures from whom the interacting characters or readers (in the case of Stein) can learn, but only through selective appropriation and translation. The influential affect between Stein and Beckett, as such, operated rather like one of Beckett's own self-translations, or the exchange of nonsense for sense that occurs between Watt and Sam throughout the passages quoted earlier, with Beckett taking Stein's crazed logography and adapting it to his own more conservative – but nonetheless still subversive – and semantically coherent setting. This setting was made fundamentally and materialistically indeterminate by Beckett's subsequent decision to split each text between two languages, creating versions of each narrative, and of each word within each narrative – insoluble logographs across and between two languages.

References

Abbott, H. Porter (2010), 'Garden Paths and Ineffable Effects: Abandoning Representation in Literature and Film', in Frederick Luis Adalma (ed.), *Towards a Cognitive Theory of Narrative Acts*, Austin: University of Texas Press, pp. 205–26.

Ackerley, C. J. (2010), *Obscure Locks, Simple Keys: The Annotated Watt*, Edinburgh: Edinburgh University Press.

Astbury, Helen (2001), 'How to Do Things with Syntax: Beckett's Binary-Turned Sentences in French and Their Translation into English', *Samuel Beckett Today/Aujourd'hui*, 11, pp. 446–53.

Banfield, Ann (1982), *Unspeakable Sentences: Narration and Representation in the Language of Fiction*, London: Routledge.

Banfield, Ann (2003), 'Beckett's Tattered Syntax', *Representations*, 84:1, pp. 6–29.

Beckett, Samuel (2001), *Disjecta: Miscellaneous Writings and a Dramatic Fragment*, ed. Ruby Cohn, London: John Calder.

Beckett, Samuel (2009a), *Company, Ill Seen Ill Said, Worstward Ho, Stirrings Still*, ed. Dirk Van Hulle, London: Faber and Faber.

Beckett, Samuel (2009b), *How It Is*, ed. Édouard Magessa O'Reilly, London: Faber and Faber.

Beckett, Samuel (2009c), *The Letters of Samuel Beckett, Vol. I: 1929–1940*, ed. Martha Dow Fehsenfeld, Lois More Overbeck, George Craig and Dan Gunn, Cambridge: Cambridge University Press.

Beckett, Samuel (2009d), *Molloy*, ed. Shane Weller, London: Faber and Faber.

Beckett, Samuel (2009e), *Texts for Nothing and Other Shorter Prose, 1950–1976*, ed. Mark Nixon, London: Faber and Faber.

Beckett, Samuel (2009f), *Watt*, ed. C. J. Ackerley, London: Faber and Faber.

Beckett, Samuel (2010), *The Unnamable*, ed. Steven Connor, London: Faber and Faber.

Beer, Ann (1985) 'Watt, Knott and Beckett's Bilingualism', *Journal of Beckett Studies*, 10, pp. 37–75.

Beer, Ann (1994), 'Beckett's Bilingualism', in John Pilling (ed.), *The Cambridge Companion to Samuel Beckett*, Cambridge: Cambridge University Press, pp. 209–21.

Carville, Conor (2018), 'Late and Belated Modernism: Duchamp ... Stein . Feininger ... Beckett', in Olga Beloborodova, Dirk Van Hulle and Pim Verhulst (eds), *Beckett and Modernism*, London: Palgrave Macmillan, pp. 53–67.

Clément, Bruno (2007), 'Logique du bilinguisme', in Chiara Montini, *'La bataille du soliloque': Genèse de la poétique bilingue de Samuel Beckett (1929–1946)*, Amsterdam: Rodopi, pp. 13–17.

Cohn, Ruby (1961), 'Samuel Beckett: Self-Translator', *PMLA*, 76, pp. 613–21.

Cohn, Ruby (1962), *Samuel Beckett: The Comic Gamut*, New Brunswick, NJ: Rutgers University Press.

Cohn, Ruby (2001), 'Foreword', in Samuel Beckett, *Disjecta: Miscellaneous Writings and a Dramatic Fragment*, ed. Ruby Cohn, London: John Calder, pp. 7–16.

Connor, Steven (1988), *Samuel Beckett: Repetition, Theory, Text*, Oxford: Basil Blackwell.

Connor, Steven (1989), 'Traduttore, traditore: Samuel Beckett's Translation of *Mercier et Camier*', *Journal of Beckett Studies*, 11–12, pp. 27–46.

Cordingley, Anthony (2007), 'Beckett and "l'ordre naturel": The Universal Grammar of *Comment c'est/How It Is*', *Samuel Beckett Today/Aujourd'hui*, 18:1, pp. 185–99.

Cordingley, Anthony, and Chiara Montini (2015), 'Genetic Translation Studies: An Emerging Discipline', *Linguistica Antverpiensia, New Series: Themes in Translation Studies*, 14. https://doi.org/10.52034/lanstts.v14i0.399. [Accessed 27 September 2021].

Coupland, Douglas (1996), *Polaroids from the Dead*, London: Flamingo.

Deeney, John F. (2013), 'Location, Location, Location: Narrative and Blankness in Recent British Drama', in David Shirley and Jane Turner (eds), *Performing Narrative: Narration, 'Denarration', Fracture and Absence in Contemporary Performance Practice*, Manchester: Manchester Metropolitan University, pp. 1–11.

Emonds, Joseph (2001), *Lexicon and Grammar: The English Syntacticon*, Berlin: Mouton De Gruyter.

Federman, Raymond (1987), 'The Writer As Self-Translator', in Alan Friedman, Charles Rossman and Dina Sherzer (eds), *Beckett Translating/ Translating Beckett*, University Park: Pennsylvania State University Press, pp. 7–16.

Fitch, Brian T. (1988), *Beckett and Babel: An Investigation into the Status of the Bilingual Work*, Toronto: University of Toronto Press.

Forsyth, Mark (2013), *The Elements of Eloquence: How to Turn the Perfect English Phrase*, London: Icon Books.

Germoni, Karine (2014), 'Play/Comédie, Come and Go/Va-et-vient, Footfalls/ Pas de Beckett; ou, Le va-et-vient de la ponctuation entre deux langues', *Samuel Beckett Today/Aujourd'hui*, 26, pp. 283–98.

Germoni, Karine, and Pascale Sardin (2012), 'Tensions of the In-Between: Rhythm, Tonelessness and Lyricism in Fin de partie/Endgame', *Samuel Beckett Today/Aujourd'hui*, 24, pp. 335–50.

Gubar, Susan (2000), *Critical Condition: Feminism at the Turn of the Century*, New York: Columbia University Press.

Hobhouse, Janet, (1975), *Everybody Who Was Anybody: A Biography of Gertrude Stein*, London: Wiedenfeld and Nicolson.

Joyce, James (2007), *Ulysses*, ed. Hans Walter Gabler, with Wolfhard Steppe and Claus Melchior, afterword by Michael Groden, London: The Bodley Head.

Kawin, Bruce F. (1972), *Telling It Again and Again: Repetition in Literature and Film*, Ithaca, NY: Cornell University Press.

Kellner, Bruce (ed.) (1988), *A Gertrude Stein Companion: Content with the Example*, New York: Greenwood Press.

Kennedy, Seán (2011), 'Beckett Publishing in Ireland 1929–1956', in Mark Nixon (ed.), *Publishing Samuel Beckett*, London: The British Library, pp. 57–71.

Knowlson, James (1997), *Damned to Fame: The Life of Samuel Beckett*, London: Bloomsbury.

Knowlson, James, with John Haynes (2003), *Images of Beckett*, Cambridge: Cambridge University Press.

Krance, Charles (ed.) (1993), *Company/Compagnie and A Piece of Monologue/ Solo: A Bilingual Variorum Edition*, New York: Garland.

Krance, Charles (ed.) (1996), *Samuel Beckett's Mal vu mal dit/Ill seen ill said: A Bilingual, Evolutionary, and Synoptic Variorum Edition*, New York: Garland.

Lodge, David (1977), *The Modes of Modern Writing: Metaphor, Metonymy, and the Typology of Modern Literature*, London: Edward Arnold.

Montini, Chiara (2007), *'La bataille du soliloque': Genèse de la poétique bilingue de Samuel Beckett (1929–1946)*, Amsterdam: Rodopi.

Montini, Chiara (2012), 'L'œuvre sans original: du brouillon à l'autotraduction et retour', in *Littérature*, 167, pp. 78–89.

Mooney, Sinéad (2010), 'Beckett in English and French', in S. E. Gontarski (ed.), *A Companion to Samuel Beckett*, Oxford: Wiley-Blackwell, pp. 196–208.

Mooney, Sinéad (2011), *A Tongue Not Mine: Beckett and Translation*, Oxford: Oxford University Press.

'New York Passenger Lists, 1820–1891', database with images, 420 – 15 Sep 1879–5 Nov 1879, image 335 of 1171; citing National Archives and Records Administration microfilm publication M237, National Archives, Washington DC. www.familysearch.org.

Nguyen, Tram (2013), Porosities: Aesthetic Correlations between Gertrude Stein and Samuel Beckett', *Samuel Beckett Today/Aujhourd'hui*, 25, pp. 45–57.

Nixon, Mark (2007), 'Beckett Publishing/Publishing Beckett in the 1930s', *Variants: Journal of the European Society for Textual Scholarship*, 6, pp. 209–19.

Nixon, Mark (2011), *Samuel Beckett's German Diaries 1936–1937*, London: Continuum.

Nugent-Folan, Georgina (2013), '"Ill Buttoned": Comparing the Representation of Objects in Samuel Beckett's *Ill Seen Ill Said* and Gertrude Stein's *Tender Buttons*', *Journal of Beckett Studies*, 22:1, pp. 54–82.

Nugent-Folan, Georgina (2015), 'Personal Apperception: Samuel Beckett, Gertrude Stein, and Paul Cézanne's *La Montagne Saint Victoire*', *Samuel Beckett Today/Aujhourd'hui*, 27:1, pp. 87–101.

Nugent-Folan, Georgina (2016), '"Say It Simply [. . .] Say It Simplier": Samuel Beckett and Gertrude Stein's Aesthetics of Writing Worser', PhD diss, University of Dublin, Trinity College.

Nugent-Folan, Georgina (2022), 'Self Re-writing and Self Un-writing: Reconsidering Gertrude Stein's Marginalisation in Discussions of Samuel Beckett's Autographic Writing', *Samuel Beckett Today/Aujhourd'hui*, 34:1, pp. 163–7.

Padgette, Paul (1971), 'Letter in Response to "*A Very Difficult Author*, from April 8, 1971"', *New York Review of Books*, 1 July. http://bit.ly/3mGzwb1 [Accessed 27 September 2021].

Perloff, Marjorie (1999), *The Poetics of Indeterminacy: Rimbaud to Cage*, Evanston, IL: Northwestern University Press.

Perloff, Marjorie (2002), *21st-Century Modernism: The 'New' Poetics*, Oxford: Blackwell.

Pilling, John, and Seán Lawlor (2011), 'Beckett in Transition', in Mark Nixon (ed.), *Publishing Samuel Beckett*, London: The British Library, pp. 83–95.

Powell, Joshua (2018), 'Gertrude Stein, Samuel Beckett and the Aesthetics of Inattention', *Samuel Beckett Today/Aujourd'hui*, 30:2, pp. 239–52.

Richardson, Brian (2001), 'Denarration in Fiction: Erasing the Story in Beckett and Others', *Narrative*, 9:2, pp. 168–75.

Sardin, Pascale (2015), 'Reading and Interpreting Variants in *Come and Go, Va-et-vient* and *Kommen und Gehen*', *Journal of Beckett Studies*, 24:1, pp. 75–86.

Sardin-Damestoy, Pascale (2002), *Samuel Beckett auto-traducteur ou l'art de 'l'empêchement': lecture bilingue et génétique des textes courts auto-traduits (1946–1980)*, Arras: Artois Presses Universitité.

Satiat, Nadine (2010), *Gertrude Stein*, Flammarion.

Scheiner, Corrine (2013), 'Self-Translation', in Anthony Uhlmann (ed.), *Samuel Beckett in Context*, Cambridge: Cambridge University Press, pp. 370–80.

Schuster, Joshua (2011), 'The Making of "Tender Buttons": Gertrude Stein's Subjects, Objects, and the Illegible', *Jacket 2*, https://jacket2.org/article/making-tender-buttons [Accessed 27 September 21].

Shirley, David, and Jane Turner (eds) (2013), *Performing Narrative: Narration, 'Denarration', Fracture and Absence in Contemporary Performance Practice*, Manchester: Manchester Metropolitan University.

Slote, Sam (2011), 'Continuing the End: Variation between Beckett's French and English Prose Works', in Mark Nixon (ed.), *Publishing Samuel Beckett*, London: The British Library, pp. 205–18.

Slote, Sam (2015), "Bilingual Beckett: Beyond the Linguistic Turn," in Dirk Van Hulle (ed.), *The New Cambridge Companion to Samuel Beckett*, Cambridge: Cambridge University Press, pp. 114–25.

Spitzer, Leo (1972), 'Une habitude de style, le rappel chez Celine', *Cahier de l'Herne: Celine*, Paris: Heme-Livre de Poche, pp. 257–73.

Stacey, Stephen (2013), 'Translating for Sense: Samuel Beckett's writing in English, French and English', Paper presented at 'Samuel Beckett and the "State" of Ireland III', University College Dublin, 3 August.

Stacey, Stephen (2018), 'Beckett and French, 1906–1946: A Study', PhD diss, University of Dublin, Trinity College.

Stein, Gertrude (1971), 'A Transatlantic Interview–1946', in Robert Bartlett Hass (ed.), *A Primer for the Gradual Understanding of Gertrude Stein*, Los Angeles: Black Sparrow Press, pp. 11–35.

Stein, Gertrude (1973), *Everybody's Autobiography*, New York: Vintage.

Stein, Gertrude (1975), *How to Write*, New York: Dover.

Stein, Gertrude (1984), *Wars I Have Seen*, New York: Random House.

Stein, Gertrude (1990), *Three Lives*, New York: Penguin.

Stein, Gertrude (1993), *Geography and Plays*, Madison: University of Wisconsin Press.

Stein, Gertrude (1995), *The Making of Americans: Being a History of a Family's Progress*, London: Dalkey Archive.

Stein, Gertrude (1996), *A Stein Reader*, ed. with an introduction by Ulla E. Dydo, Evanston, IL: Northwestern University Press.

Stein, Gertrude (1998), *Writings 1932–1946*, New York: Library of America.

Stein, Gertrude (2001), *The Autobiography of Alice B. Toklas*, London: Penguin.

Stein, Gertrude (2003), *Paris, France*, London: Peter Owen.

Stein, Gertrude (2004), *Look At Me Now and Here I Am: Selected Works 1911–1945*, ed. Patricia Meyerowitz, London: Peter Owen.

Stein, Gertrude (2010), *Narration*, Chicago, IL: University of Chicago Press.

Stein, Gertrude (2014), *Tender Buttons: The Corrected Centennial Edition*, San Francisco: City Lights.

Taylor-Batty, Juliet (2013), *Multilingualism in Modernist Fiction*, Basingstoke: Palgrave Macmillan.

The Oxford English Dictionary (2021), Third Edition. http://dictionary.oed.com.

Van Hulle, Dirk (2014), 'The Obidil and the Man of Glass: Denarration, Genesis and Cognition in Beckett's *Molloy, Malone meurt/Malone Dies* and *L'innommable/The Unnamable'*, *Samuel Beckett Today/Aujourd'hui*, 26:1, pp. 25–39.

Van Hulle, Dirk, and Mark Nixon (2013), *Samuel Beckett's Library*, Cambridge: Cambridge University Press.

Van Hulle, Dirk, and Shane Weller (2014), *The Making of Samuel Beckett's L'innommable/The Unnamable*. The Beckett Digital Manuscript Project 02, London: Bloomsbury.

Weller, Shane (2021), *Samuel Beckett and Cultural Nationalism*, Cambridge: Cambridge University Press.

Wilson, Robert A. (1974), *Gertrude Stein: A Bibliography*, New York: Phoenix Bookshop.

Wineapple, Brenda (2008), *Sister Brother: Gertrude and Leo Stein*, Lincoln: University of Nebraska Press.

Cambridge Elements ≡

Beckett Studies

Dirk Van Hulle
University of Oxford
Dirk Van Hulle is Professor of Bibliography and Modern Book History at the University of Oxford and director of the Centre for Manuscript Genetics at the University of Antwerp.

Mark Nixon
University of Reading
Mark Nixon is Associate Professor in Modern Literature at the University of Reading and the Co-director of the Beckett International Foundation.

About the Series
This series presents cutting-edge research by distinguished and emerging scholars, providing space for the most relevant debates informing Beckett studies as well as neglected aspects of his work. In times of technological development, religious radicalism, unprecedented migration, gender fluidity, environmental and social crisis, Beckett's works find increased resonance. Cambridge Elements in Beckett Studies is a key resource for readers interested in the current state of the field.

Cambridge Elements ≡

Beckett Studies

Elements in the Series

Printed in the United States
by Baker & Taylor Publisher Services